The
PROGRESSED
HOROSCOPE
SIMPLIFIED
by
LEIGH HOPE MILBURN

∽

⨍⨍⨍

∽

First Printing 1928
Current Printing 1989
ISBN Number: 0-86690-131-0

Cover Design: Lynda Kay Fullerton

Published by:
American Federation of Astrologers, Inc.
P.O. Box 22040, 6535 South Rural Road
Tempe, Arizona 85285-2040

Printed in the United States of America

Dedication

TO MY HUSBAND
WITHOUT WHOSE SYMPATHY AND CO-OPERATION
THIS BOOK COULD NOT HAVE
BEEN WRITTEN

Preface to Third Edition

The continued interest of students of astrology in Leigh Hope Milburn's "The Progressed Horoscope Simplified" has necessitated this third printing.

When the first edition was published in 1928, Llewellyn George, in an introduction, said: "Mrs. Milburn has had a wealth of experience in progressed horoscope work, both during her seven years' connection with the Llewellyn College of Astrology and in her active class work. Therefore, "The Progressed Horoscope Simplified" will convey to students of astrology practical information for delineating such horoscopes in actual practice and, as such, will be a valuable contribution to astrological literature.

In this new edition the author has corrected some small errors that appear in the second edition and has added two new paragraphs to page 87.

November, 1936.

PLATE 1.

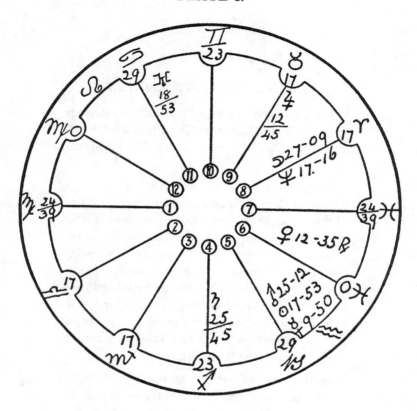

NATIVITY.
Male, born February 6, 1870, at 8:24 p. m.
Latitude, 51.30 North. Longitude, 2. West.

PLATE 2.

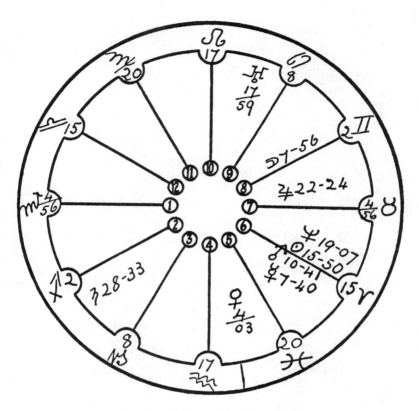

PROGRESSED HOROSCOPE.
Male, born February 6, 1870, at 8:24 p. m.
Progressed birth date, April 5, 1870.

Table of Contents

The Progressed Horoscope Simplified

CHAPTER 1.

PROGRESSED HOROSCOPE DEFINED.

In Genethliacal or Natal Astrology the Radical Horoscope is a chart or map showing the position of the planets, relative to each other and the signs, at the time of birth.

The Progressed Horoscope shows the positions of the planets, relative to each other and the signs, at some particular time subsequent to birth.

The Natal Horoscope indicates influences that play on or through the native at the time of birth and those that will do so at subsequent periods, but it does not indicate at what particular times in his life any particular influence, or set of influences, will become more potent or less potent.

The Progressed Horoscope indicates—for that particular time for which it is set up—the relative activity of the influences indicated in the Natal Chart. It should not be studied solely with the idea of being able to change those conditions, even though we may consider them unfavorable. But, rather, that we may be prepared to meet them with the right spirit and thus reach, from the right direction, the goal for which we are set. Predictions can be made in a general way, right through life, from birth until death, though the finer details have to be omitted until an ephemeris for the current year is available.

The Progressed Horoscope represents the most difficult section of the science of Astrology. The reading of the Radical Horoscope may be likened to the first lessons in music, where notes for only one finger at a time are usual, as in scales and simple exercises, and the Progressed Horoscope to the more advanced music where one is dealing with chords and many complicated notes. Yet, as in music, it is upon a

(9)

clear comprehension of the rudiments that a knowledge of the more advanced steps rests. It is quite hopeless for a person to try to read a Progressed Horoscope unless he is able to delineate that which is promised at the time of birth, and the conditions under which the native of the horoscope is working.

It is naturally the ambition of every beginner to be able to read the future as indicated by the Progressed Horoscope; just as every child, beginning music, yearns to be able to play tunes. But to reach either goal means hard work and study, plus time and experience, and it can be attained only by this method.

Those influences in the Progressed Horoscope showing indications contrary to what is promised in the Radical Chart cannot deeply affect the native, but many things can, and do, happen which we, with our limited knowledge of Astrology, fail to see indicated in the Natal Chart. Let us make the first statement a little clearer and then take up the second. Supposing, in a Radical Chart, Venus were situated in the eleventh house making a sextile to the Sun; this would indicate many friends, pleasures and happiness through them, and many women companions. Therefore, even if, in the Progressed Chart, the Sun or Venus were making adverse aspects to either of these planets in the Natal Chart, it would have no adverse effect, but might even prove a beneficial influence for these things, because the aspect would be acting as a current along which the benefits promised might pass. But let us suppose at the same time that Venus was making an adverse aspect to Saturn at the time of birth—that would indicate that at some time in the life there would be disappointments through, or death of, friends, or many delays and annoyances caused by them, depending upon the position of Saturn on the map. Thus, at the time that Venus or Saturn, in the Progressed Horoscope, are found making aspects to either of these planets in the Natal Horoscope, especially to Venus, would be the time that those things promised by this position of Venus and Saturn would manifest.

Regarding the statement that things happen that are not seen in the Natal Chart—by that we mean that, as the influences come into play, there is nothing to prohibit them from having an effect, by anything to the contrary in the Radical Horoscope, and just to the extent that we are responding to any particular aspects, just so much will they influence us either for good or evil according to the nature of the influence.

Many people respond to every vibration that comes into their radius; some respond only to the lower vibrations, and others only to the higher ones, while the rest remain stationary, as it were, responding only to the vibrations which have been playing upon them from the time of their birth. These latter make practically no progress during an incarnation and correspond to the "lukewarm" type. The others are making progress of some kind, but few of us make the progress that we should, and could, with the right understanding and use of Astrology.

Reduced to its simplest form of expression, everything is vibration, and it is reasonable to assume that every vibration in the Solar System affects us to a greater or lesser extent, just as any special noise (or vibration), close at hand, can affect us, according to whether it is a pleasing or objection-able noise, or the sounds (of which we may be scarcely aware) which come from the city or locality in which we may be residing also affect us. We know how readily we respond to the rays of the Sun and Moon, so that it should not be difficult to assume that the rest of the planets also have an effect upon us. The Solar System is a great body and the planets, including the Earth, are its organs, so that there must be a very close link between them all, and as in the physical body, the disorder of one organ has the power to upset and disarrange any or all of the others. The ancients knew the basic principles of Astrology and went so far as to explain a correspondence between the planets and all other things in nature—to metals, plants, colors, etc., showing the knowledge they had of the intimate relationship of our planets to one another and to everything else in the Solar System.

Assuming, then, that we all understand and accept this, we may proceed to study the effects of the influences of these planets in their different combinations. Many books have already been written explaining the effects of the positions of the planets in the different signs of the Zodiac and their relations to one another, so that we will not take the time here for that part of the science, but will endeavor to explain the way the combinations of vibrations work, when the planets begin to progress and the native responds to them.

We find, as we look among our friends, that there are some who seem to respond very little to conditions and progress that is going on around them; that they stay in the same set ways, hold the same kind of thoughts and rarely venture upon an original idea. They live in a little circle, getting up every morning about the same time, eat much the same morning meal, remain in the same occupation for many years, read the newspapers, play cards and go to the movies and retire without having made any noticeable progress, excepting in so far as nature has forced upon them certain experiences through which they are obliged to live. And even these will often leave them more stunned than awakened, more questioning and bitter than realizing and grateful. And so we find at the end of life they have made so little advancement (unless it is in material things) that their lives appear to have been utterly wasted. These are the people who respond but very little to the influences of the planets in their progression. Then there are others who respond to every vibration that plays upon them. They are torn and swept by every emotion that touches them, they are easily angered, easily excited, nervous, high-strung and temperamental. Those of this type usually consider they are making great progress, that they are getting much out of life, and living in the only way worth while. The former belong to the fixed signs—generally speaking—and the latter to the cardinal. Next we come to the mutable sign type. They are mental and thoughtful and respond in such manner to the influences as they continually play upon them. They are interested in the "why" of the vibrations; they are anxious to get at the root of life and to learn more of the secrets of nature, and therefore they are the ones who respond more fully, and in the right way, to the progressed influences.

CHAPTER 2.

GENERAL APPLICATION.

There are a great many things to be taken into consideration when one begins to predict from a Progressed Horoscope. First, it is well to have some knowledge of the lines of least resistance. By that we mean in which particular direction the influences from any given sign, house or aspect are affecting the native whose chart is being considered. Each sign and each house represents, or indicates, many things. For instance, the third house represents brothers and sisters, short journeys, the lower mind and all kinds of secretarial work. Very well, we will suppose that we have the chart of a person who does no work with his pen, has no relatives and is not in a position to take any journeys. We find in his Progressed Chart that Jupiter is transiting over the Sun in the third house. This could mean that he would make a short journey which would be exceedingly beneficial, or that he would receive some special advantage or gain through relatives, or that he might receive benefit, promotion or unusually good opportunities in the position of salesman, secretary or similar work, or else through writing. But in regard to the supposed person under discussion—since most of these doors are closed for him—this benefic conjunction would work on the mental plane, making him much more buoyant, raising his thoughts to higher planes, lifting him out of the rut of usual thought and turning it to lines of philosophy, law or some of the higher sciences, and would draw out many latent possibilities, that he may not even have known were there. This would be due to the influence of Jupiter working through his own natural line of ninth house affairs, playing upon the Sun, which represents the individuality and all that lies therein, whether being demonstrated on the material plane or not. This third house being one of the houses ruling the mind, it is quite possible for a person to traverse new ground of thought instead of taking a journey on the physical plane, for in all instances the influences will work on one plane or another, and because a person is looking for any particular influence to operate in a certain way, and fails

(13)

to see it, does not mean that it has passed by altogether, for it will assuredly be operating on some plane even if the person is not quick enough to perceive it. The art is in being able to tell, from the type of horoscope, and what one knows of that native's life, just how the given influences will work out. We are all subject to all the effects of all the influences, and only when we are, as St. Paul says, "Above the Law," will we not be subject to the conditions under which we have to work.

However, the influences are merely open doors through which we should be able to step with ease to the experiences awaiting us beyond; and whether the experience will prove to be painful or not depends entirely upon the attitude of mind with which we come prepared to meet it. The influence will be there and we will respond to it; but the question is, in what way shall it be? Good aspects can be just as evil in a sense, in their effects, as those which we consider adverse, for they, too, contain a lesson and a test, and if we cannot meet the prosperity or benefits which they bring, in the right spirit, then the results will bring us under evil influences and we will have much to do over again.

Therefore, what is known as a fortunate horoscope, from the worldly point of view, may have just the reverse effect and be the means of a person's complete undoing.

The study of the Progressed Horoscope is an intricate one and can only be done successfully after one has mastered the science of reading a Natal Chart. Too often do we find the student desiring to do this advanced work before he is in any way capable of understanding it. Too seldom do we find the student who is willing to grind his way up to the progressed work, and who is willing to get the right foundation for what he has to do later or who understands the true basis of Astrology. As we have said, this is a complicated affair, for there are at least three charts to be taken into consideration. First, there is the progression of the signs, which is called primary direction; second, there is the natural progression of the planets themselves, called secondary direction, and, third, there are the planets as they are in the heavens at any given time and used under the title of "Transits" and all these three are to be used in connection with the Natal Chart itself.

The Progressed Chart is set up in the following manner: First, we must find the progressed birthday, which is done by calculating one day for every year after birth, taking Chart No. 1 as our example. The birth day is February 6, 1870, and this is the year 1928, making the native 58 years of age. Add 58 days to the date of birth and it brings us to April 5th as being the progressed birthday for February 6, 1928. Then the chart is set up for this day in exactly the same manner as it was for the day of his actual birth. Chart No. 2 will illustrate this. The same latitude and longitude must be used as are given for the place of birth.

There are two other methods for setting up the wheel for the primary directions. One is, to add as many degrees to the mid-heaven as the native is years old, that is to say, one degree for every year, and setting up the chart from this point, the remainder is filled in from the Table of Houses in the regular manner, using the Sidereal time that is represented by the degree found on the progressed mid-heaven. The other method is to add to the ascendant as many degrees, minutes and seconds as the Sun has moved from the day of birth to the progressed birth date, taking, as before, one day for every year.

Then (and this applies to all three methods) the planets' places are calculated on the progressed birthday just the same as though that were the Natal Chart, the same logarithm being used as on the birth day. We will now use the illustration that we have started upon by which to illustrate much of what is necessary in this progressed work. Of course we cannot demonstrate all conditions in so few illustrations and so small a work, but the general principles will apply in most cases and the rest is left to the student's own intuition and ability to synthesize.

To get a better understanding of the progressed delineation from this chart it will be well to give a rough outline of what is indicated in the nativity, for, as has already been said, no vibrations have the same effect when operating in the Progressed Chart which do not find a response in the native's own character or tendencies or experiences. The male whose life is represented by this chart was born when the 25th degree of Virgo was rising upon the ascendant with Gemini 23 on the mid-heaven. Virgo is a mental sign and of the mutable quality.

You will remember what has been said of the general way in which the different types respond to the progressing vibrations—well, this is a very good illustration. The mutable signs here rule all the angles, while the ruler of the chart, Mercury (ruler of both the Mid-Heaven and the Ascendant), the Sun, ruling the individuality, and the pioneering planet Mars are all in the mental, intuitive sign of Aquarius. You would therefore find that this man does not take life lightly, that the perception and criticism indicated by the rising sign are used for every phase and condition of life; therefore he advances in thought as the planets progress.

The Sun in Aquarius makes him thoughtful, keen to understand and to get the very best interpretations out of life. Nothing short of perfection in all things will suit him, whether perfection is necessary or not. His desire is for knowledge and advancement as seen by the mental signs ruling the ascendant and mid-heaven and the sign of science and research (Aquarius) holding three important planets and Uranus (ruler of Aquarius), the most elevated planet in the map. Virgo being a practical, industrious sign, he would never be idle and the inventive original sign Aquarius would give him the desire to improve everything with which he had anything to do, especially when we take into account the elevation of the ruler of this sign Uranus, so that the general tone of this chart is towards progression and perfection. Thus it will be readily understood that the progression of the planets in this case should have the desired effect, that of evolution of mind and soul, though doubtless at the expense of the physical body.

An earthy sign rising and so many planets in fixed signs indicates good health as a whole, with plenty of resistance and reserve, but the onslaught of Saturn to the ascendant, which is made by his square aspect to that point from the fourth house, will tend, every seven years, to overthrow him and to cause more or less serious illness. We say every seven years, because Saturn's cycle is approximately 29 years and that brings him to a square, opposition or conjunction of his own radical place and of the radical ascendant approximately every seven years and thus excites into action the things promised by this configuration at the time of birth.

A happy marriage is indicated by the sextile of the love planet, Venus, and Jupiter the greater benefic, Venus being in the sign ruling, and posited not far from the cusp of, the seventh house, which is the house of marriage. Neptune is the ruler of this sign and is in Aries at the time of birth, and it was when he came, by primary direction, to the cusp of the seventh house, and the Sun, also by primary direction, making a trine to the ascendant, at the age of 32 years, that he became engaged, marrying when the Sun was sextile the progressed seventh cusp, by direction. The girl had Neptune rising in Taurus, thus giving the mixture of Neptune and Venus, the latter being the ruler of Taurus, that shows so plainly in his own chart. The ruler of the girl's chart, Venus, fell in conjunction with his Sun in Aquarius, which was the sign ruling her mid-heaven. The strong Uranian and Aquarian vibrations of both charts caused them to take up in all seriousness many occult lines of thought.

This is not a fortunate chart for material gain or wealth, for in no case when the Sun has set, that is, when he is placed between the seventh and fourth houses, is there much opportunity for the exercise of free will and this is made more evident by the sign of service that is rising upon the ascendant, a sign that belongs to a cadent house. So this man, while having more than the average ability in many directions, has not been able to use it for any material success. The position and aspects of the Sun also bear this out, for the Sun has just passed the square to Jupiter, the bountiful giver of this world's goods, while he is making a sextile to Neptune and a quincunx (150 degrees), which is a very occult aspect, to Uranus, both of which point the way to occultism and to spiritual lines of operation rather than material ones. Therefore, it is clear that this was the requirement of his soul and the point to which he has now advanced, and only by a strict denial of material wealth, and by handicaps and obstacles indicated by the square of Saturn to the ascendant, could he take up the other lines.

Thus, in making predictions for this person one would need to bear all this in mind and understand on which planes to place the results of the progressed influences. Whenever there are any aspects of Venus the effects will be good, or, at any rate, not evil, even though the aspects be adverse. Whenever Jupiter makes an aspect to Venus he will open the door for good to come because of the promise of the good natal aspect, and whenever there is an aspect of Jupiter or the Sun to each other the effect will tend to be for loss and difficulty rather than for benefit. As, for instance, the conjunction of Jupiter with the Sun has been known to bring practically no results unless it might be some slight improvement to the health.

Again, it should be remembered that in such a sensitive organism as this all aspects of the impulsive Mars, the changeable Moon and the mental planet Mercury will have an effect upon the nervous system and set the nerves aquiver, as it were, and if the aspects are adverse the effects will be accordingly and only with difficulty will poise be maintained. All persons with mutable signs rising, or dominant, are temperamental and nervous, and so the planets just mentioned, Mars, the Moon and Mercury (together with Neptune and Uranus if they are afflicted), will continually cause eruption or disruption according to the general tenor of the Radical Chart. All cardinal signs show a high-strung nature, restless and keen, and therefore all aspects will tend to excite these characteristics, the good aspects being naturally helpful, if the chart is favorable enough for the good to have sufficient influence; and the evil aspects will cause excitement, rashness and activity to the detriment of the native according to the possibilities of the nativity. With the fixed signs it is quite different—just the opposite in fact. Aspects have not the same quick effect; such persons are more stolid and not easily moved and do not respond to any aspects as quickly, even though they are of the nature to awaken those things that are promised by the position and aspects in the Natal Chart.

The question of synthesis is a very subtle one and cannot be understood without training the intuition. Astrology as a science comes under the rule of Uranus, and this planet is the one through which we get our intuition, so that the development of the one goes hand in hand with the other. There is no intention to moralize in this work, but it may be said here, with benefit to the student, that only he who makes an earnest study of this great occult science for the sake of the science and for knowledge alone, and not for any personal gain or advantage that he may derive, can become a good astrologer with a steady development of the intuition which is so necessary. To go back to the point of synthesis, let us take the illustration of Chart No. 1 again. Here we find the sign of service rising, with the ruler in the great humanitarian sign Aquarius, together with the planet that rules the individuality and also the planet of progress and ambition, Mars. The ideals of such a person are naturally very high, and with Uranus elevated above everything else and in a watery sign, the intuition is well developed, so that when there are afflictions in the Progressed Chart they do not affect him as they would a person of less development. And when we find such an influence as Uranus transiting back and forth over the opposite point of the ascendant, instead of this man going to pieces with nervous trouble, or causing trouble or separation with his partners, marital or otherwise, through sudden fits of temper and irritation, we find him using it as an opportunity for testing his strength of will and resistance, and thus, responding to the Uranian influence upon the higher planes, he develops more intuition and a better understanding of all occult truths. With a lower type of horoscope this affliction could very easily have caused a complete nervous breakdown, or an estrangement between the native and his wife, for in the Radical Chart Uranus has an affliction from the Sun and is in the sign which represents the home, while Saturn afflicts from the house of the home.

CHAPTER 3.

PREDOMINANCE OF THE PLANETS.

It is usually found that, by progression, one or more planets are more dominant either by position or aspects than others and therefore the whole year is tinged, so to speak, with the nature of that planet or planets. As, for instance, if it is Mars that is dominant, then his enthusiasm and energy will permeate and affect even the slow and deliberate operations of Saturn and cause more stir in all the events and conditions and impart to all the other planets something of his own nature. And likewise, if it were Saturn that held the greatest power for the year, everything would be slower and more deliberate, with greater restraint and less spontaniety and buoyancy. Though, of course, the general tendency of the Radical Chart would have to be considered, for it would take a great deal of Saturn to hold back the natural vitality and impulse as seen in some nativities. The most it will do in such cases is to cause quietness in spots, as it were, with sudden rushes of the old energy in between.

The Sun.

When the Sun is strongest, by aspect, in the Progressed Chart it indicates that there are important experiences awaiting the individual. These experiences extend over a period of not less than three years, and sometimes longer, the reason being explained elsewhere in this work. These solar influences are for the purpose of developing the soul and are usually very powerful, and when the aspects are adverse, often it is all a person can do to stand up under the force of the vibrations that are pouring upon him. But it surely does develop the character, and when one understands what one has to meet, and is primed for the battle, one is able to face it with the right attitude of mind through a knowledge of Astrology, so that much of the pain is eliminated. The idea is to bring out individual characteristics, to teach us to become less personal, to view things from a larger standpoint, to get more in touch with other egos and that which is back of their actions, mannerisms and idiosyncrasies and to pay less attention to the superficial as is displayed in the personality.

The Moon.

When the Moon is important in the directions, it tends to act in just the opposite manner from the Sun. We find all things of a personal nature coming to the fore. All conditions and events will be applied in terms of the personality and the immediate environment will be disturbed either for good or ill according to the nature of the aspects, and those conditions which closely surround the person will be the most directly affected and thus affect the native. Events will apply more in the home and in the daily life rather than having a larger and deeper meaning and effect. The Moon brings petty details and events that have only a passing significance, and thus a year that is dominated by the Moon may be full of little annoyances and small changes for the most part with little meaning, to the end that the year will be one which passes quickly but with little to show for it.

Mercury.

When Mercury has the greatest dominance, then all the mental side of the nature is stirred. There will be the desire to read, write, take up new studies and to work with all those things in which correspondence, documents, lecturing, literary work of any kind are necessary. There will be something of the same restlessness and change that the Moon tends to bring, but will make for more adaptability, cooperation and travel. The dominance of this planet will bring a greater tension on the nervous system, keener perception and greater sensitiveness.

Venus.

If there are many Venus aspects, then the native will incline more to pleasures and association with friends and to the arts. All things of beauty will have a greater appeal and one will naturally turn more towards those things which stir the feelings and emotions. For Venus rules love and affection, whether between the opposite sexes or those of the same sex, and when this planet has dominance there is a greater desire for expression in this manner and her rule always brings a period when one will turn to one's friends for love, sympathy and pleasures.

Mars.

With Mars dominant in the directions it is more difficult to control the actions, for desire and impulse will now be strong and, in the case of the ungoverned ego, these will tend to overrule everything else. But to the progressive individual it will bring force and energy that may be used to great advantage. In either case there will be more passion, positiveness, self-reliance and ambition and it will depend upon the nature of the individual as to how these are used. There are some who have their lower natures so well in hand that the Mars vibrations are used only in the most constructive ways. For instance, one man who had Mars progressed to a conjunction of Neptune and the ascendant at the same time was practically undisturbed inwardly, showed no signs of temperament or passion and was able to meet all events with calmness and dispassion. The only way it appeared to work out was in the practice of some deception against him, and since he was able to take this in the right attitude, it, too, worked out to his ultimate benefit and brought a change of location and conditions that were a distinct improvement. Not only that, but a good deal of inspiration and realization came to him that could not have been obtained had he been swayed by the violence and tumult that this force could bring to a less developed individual. This would not have worked out so well if the aspect had been a square instead of a conjunction.

Jupiter.

When Jupiter is prominent in the directions we look for an expansion in all things. There will be more sociability, hopefulness and harmony; more activity along philanthropic lines and a general upliftment of all things to a higher plane. When Jupiter's aspects are good, then one's conditions take on the air they would if a rich uncle had just come home. Of course, if the directions are not good, then the expansion will bring about loss, poor judgment and various troubles, depending upon the nature of the aspects.

Saturn.

When Saturn is important in the Progressed Chart there will be the reverse of the Jupiterian influence. For his action is to draw in, to contract and to concentrate all the affairs of life to one focusing point and to hold all activities back so that we can take time to consider what has already been done and profit thereby. Jupiter, on the one hand, brings an expansion of feeling, friendship and sociability, whereas Saturn does the reverse. He tends towards coldness, selfishness, isolation, reserve and economy.

Uranus.

The effect of Uranus dominant in the directions is to bring the unexpected. His actions tend to create upheavals, to destroy existing conditions and to bring about events so suddenly that one has no time to hold back their tide. His lesson is detachment—that we should learn to be willing to give up what we have in order to get something better. We so often get to the state of the monkey who is trapped by placing something tempting inside a container with a small opening. When he grasps the prize he cannot draw out his hand and he cannot bear to let it go, and thus sacrifices his freedom for something that he cannot use anyway. That is the way with us. Uranus would lead us to freedom of thought and action and liberate our souls. But left to ourselves, we would never give up what we already have. We take for our motto: "Better the devil you know than the devil you don't know"— not realizing that maybe it is the god that is awaiting us outside the bonds.

Neptune.

When the Neptunian influence is the most dominant, it is much more difficult to tell how things are going to be because of the uncertainty of the individual in his response to this most mystical planet. In some it produces chaotic conditions; in others it has little or no effect, and on still another group it gives greater desire for psychism and mysticism. It increases the imagination and the sensitiveness of the native and brings about weird events and contacts with unusual people. When the aspects are adverse, there is danger of treachery, theft and scandal. And no matter what the aspects, there is usually some travel, removals or change.

The action of the planets in their progression differs with each individual and each individual differs at the various stages of life according to the extent of his previous experiences and lessons, sometimes working on one plane and sometimes on another. If one is very spiritually minded, many things may happen on the material plane which would have no effect upon such a person at all, while another, with his mind centered upon material things, may be terribly upset by some very small happening. We have all seen how some people can be annoyed and spend a sleepless night over some thing to which another would never give a second thought; so that such a person seems to absorb only the evil and overlook the good almost entirely. We have heard people say that they do not see why it is only the evil directions that affect them, while the good ones pass them by. Such is never the case. It remains entirely with the individual as to how much of the one or the other he may extract from what should really be nothing but experience; and without much feeling one way or the other. As a matter of fact, we all get far more than twice the good that we do of the bad from the influences and progression of the planets if we would only stop to realize it.

Generally speaking, Venus and Jupiter (the two benefics) bring us all our blessings, and Mars and Saturn (the so-called malefics) bring the trials and problems. Venus travels through the Zodiac at about twice the speed of Mars and thus contacts her openings for benefit much oftener than Mars does for his evil influences. And Jupiter travels at twice the speed of Saturn, so that we get a similar effect from these two, as in the case of Venus and Mars. And yet so little do we appreciate the good things, that we constantly overlook this fact. There are many who go to an astrologer only at the times when things are going against them. They forget to acknowledge the times when things are going well, so much do they take their benefits for granted. It should be remembered, however, that if a Natal Chart is naturally a much afflicted one the good directions of Venus and Jupiter will be very much less effective than they will be in a Normal Chart, and the reverse will be true—that the malefics will have much more power.

Taking an ordinary chart, however, the following will stand as written. When the Moon makes or receives many aspects during any given year, there will be a general inclination towards change. The mind will be more restless and there will be the feeling that one must be up and doing, and the actions will be according to the nature of the planet aspected. For instance, an aspect to Saturn will give a desire to put one's affairs in order, to make a will, to tidy a closet or to attend generally to one's duties. An aspect to Venus will induce visiting, fun, music and love-making—while with Mercury one will get busy with one's correspondence, or take a journey, and so on.

All lives are worked out through lessons and tests, and it is exceedingly interesting to note how the horoscope works out in this plan. To explain: Let us take Chart No. 1. Here we find the Sun square to Jupiter, which, the reader will find in the text-books, usually brings financial difficulties, bad luck and many reversals in business. But at the age of 25 years the Sun progressed to a sextile with Jupiter and thus gave the native the opportunity of experiencing some affluence and good fortune, though of course not abundantly, and so brought a new test and experience such as he had not been given before. Then, also, the Sun was quincunx to Uranus at the time of birth, a rather unsettling and disturbing influence, especially for business affairs and friendships, but at the age of 31 years the Sun came into trine with this planet and brought a period of business success and also contact with the girl whom he eventually married.

Yet another instance: The Sun in the Radical Chart is forming a sextile with Saturn, which is a help to success in life through one's own efforts and efficiency. But at the age of 38 years (and extending over a period of many years, till the Sun passed the square of the progressed Saturn) the Sun arrived at the square of the radical Saturn and so brought a period when his health was poor and when the opportunities were too few to give him the chance to succeed by his own efforts and brought hampering conditions of all kinds that made progress almost impossible.

Thus all the time there is this constant testing out, first one way and then the other, just as the pendulum of the clock swings to and fro; a changing of vibrations and experiences, and it is only the very well-balanced person who is able to come through calm and undisturbed. The same thing applies to the progression of all the planets and also to their transits, as we have just described of the Sun. Constantly they are changing and playing upon one from different angles, so that we have opportunities for all kinds of experiences and should eventually be able to adjust ourselves to any condition without distress or complaint. The danger of taking the wrong attitude towards the events of life is to make us selfish and self-absorbed, and this may be brought about just as easily, if not more so, by too much good fortune. Therefore the good aspects do not always have the beneficial effect that is usually expected of them.

In considering the adverse aspects the square is the only really hard one. This influence usually brings the "fate" and it is almost impossible to divert the vibrations that will flow from this angle. Nothing can be done but to bear up under the afflictions as well as possible. But the conjunction and opposition are different. They are, as it were, open doors, and always bring us as much opportunity as adversity. They may be applied in just the same way as open doors on the physical plane. If we stand in the draught and take the full force of the current of air, we lay ourselves open to taking cold; but if we stand aside and allow the current to air the rooms, then we have not only avoided trouble but at the same time been greatly refreshed.

The square represents the cross and is the only aspect which brings the burdens over which we apparently have no control in this incarnation. The aspects of the progressed planets and transits are more potent and forceful when applied to the Radical Chart than to the Progressed Chart. When apply-

ing the progression and transits of the planets to the Radical
Chart they should be read right into that chart. That is to
say, they form for the time being a part of the nativity and
are read as though they were in those houses and signs in
which they fall in the Natal Chart. When the aspects are
applying to the progressed planets, they are read in terms of
the Progressed Chart and have their effect in the houses and
signs of the progressed figure, with its changed ascendant
and positions.

No aspects should be considered when they are more than
a full degree away, unless we except the Sun when he is
approaching a powerful aspect or when he is passing from a
radical position of some planet to that planet's progressed
place; in which case he keeps the conditions operating that
are brought about by the first aspect, though having more
power at the times when the aspects are exact, gradually
changing, however, in action according to the positions of the
radical and progressed places. Thus, we will suppose that the
Sun is making a square to Uranus in the seventh house in the
Radical Chart. This would naturally bring about a separation, divorce or estrangement with the marriage or business
partner, or both, according to the conditions of the life, and
these unsettled and unhappy conditions would be kept alive all
the time the Sun was progressing from the radical Uranus
until it came to the progressed Uranus, which of course would
not be a great distance, just a degree or two at most, taking
a corresponding number of years. But by the time it gets
to the progressed planet the effects will be somewhat different,
since (we will say) Uranus would be in the sixth house of the
Progressed Chart, and therefore the main result would be to
the health, thus making it quite safe to predict that ill-health
would follow the separations and troubles with the partner
unless the native took considerable care of himself and guarded
against excitement and nervousness. With the other planets
the same thing will occur to a lesser extent, though the
quick-moving planets will act only when the aspects are exact.
The transits of the slower moving planets—Saturn, Uranus
and Neptune—act more like directions and have very much
the same effect, for they will hover near a planet sometimes

for months at a time when they are slowing up, either to retrograde or to turn direct again. In fact, with Neptune, the influence may easily last for a couple of years, if not more.

The progressed Moon, uninfluenced by other conditions, will operate only at the time when the aspect is exact, but when there is the influence of some major transiting planet it will often hasten or delay her action at any particular period. The same thing may be said of the parallels. They begin to operate within a degree and last for a considerable period, as their motion is very slow. The parallel position of the Moon is found and worked out in the same manner as is the progressed Moon.

If one planet forms a parallel to another planet to which it is also making some other aspect, or which had an aspect at the time of birth, then the progressed parallel takes on the nature of that aspect, and is good or evil in effect accordingly. Usually the effect is to intensify the nature of the planets. For instance, a parallel of Mars to Mercury will accentuate the mental faculties, making the native keener and more alert, and if the radical tendency is such, will cause him to be more nervous and highly strung.

In the case of the Sun it frequently happens that he will make a parallel to a planet some years before making an aspect to that same planet and the parallel will act as is the nature of the forming aspect, and the whole influence will extend until the aspect is complete, sometimes extending over a great many years. Again the same thing applies to all the other planets.

In estimating the influence of progressions and transits, it must be borne in mind that whatever aspects any planet may make, whether favorable or unfavorable, it will stir into activity in *some* measure the influence denoted by its aspects in the nativity, even though the influence by progression is of a contrary nature to that in the nativity. For instance, Saturn, afflicted in the nativity, will be stirred into activity by any aspect to this planet by progression, even though the progressed aspect is a favorable one, so that the native will experience during the period over which the progressed aspect is active not only the benefic influence of the progressed aspect but the adverse influence of the natal aspect.

In such a case as this, where the planet is a malefic, the adverse influence of the nativity brought out under a favorable progression will be sufficiently strong to be noticed, but if, instead of the malefic Saturn, his place in the Natal Chart were occupied by Venus, her adverse natal influence would be excited to a lesser degree by a benefic progression, so slight as to be negligible and might well pass unnoticed.

CHAPTER 4.

THE NATURE AND INFLUENCE OF THE PLANETS.

It is essential for one to have a fundamental knowledge of the natural influences of the planets in order to make predictions and tell how, in the main, they will work under any given circumstances. Mercury and the Sun are the planets of greatest importance in delineating a Progressed Horoscope, for the former dominates the thought and the latter the individuality, and it is the inner man (the individual) and his thought which decides the actions. Mercury pertains to the things of a mental nature and so all aspects to this planet will tend to affect the mentality in some way according to the nature of the planet that is making the aspect, for Mercury is like the chamelion and takes its color and character from the planet most closely connected with it. The intelligence will be aroused according to the strength of the contacts, and under fortunate directions all the things which are governed by Mercury will be more satisfactory. For instance, aspected with Jupiter the mind will be more expansive, more benign and more satisfied, while the judgment will be more reliable.

Or again, when Mercury is connected with Saturn, the mind will work slower, but will be steadier and more sure in its reasoning and work done under this influence will be more enduring and reliable. With Mars the mind will act rather too quickly; the native will be too eager to act, but will be mentally very perceptive and keen, grasping things at a glance and working with promptness and agility. When Mercury is connected with Venus one comes into a more peaceful, soft and tender frame of mind. There will be a greater kindliness and lovingness and an increased desire for music, art, pleasures and the luxuries of life.

If Mercury is connected with the Moon, there will be a tendency to change in habits, thoughts and ideas; a desire to travel and to make alterations; and when Mercury is connected with the Sun the thought will be stronger and more egotistical or, perhaps we should say, more individual; and there will be sufficient mental dominance to increase the skill in handling people and to make one more adaptable to circumstances. Considering Uranus in connection with Mercury, the mind will show less stability as regards material things, and will be more erratic and uncertain. Yet, at the same time it will be more intuitional and original and, when taken with Neptune, the planet which connects up with the higher planes, there will be inspiration, spiritual thought, an increase of the artistic and creative faculties and a greater inclination to the esthetic side of life.

At all times Mercury takes color from the planet that is at the time influencing him, and when there is more than one, the difference in the influences will be just as apparent, though not so much a blending of the vibrations as showing themselves at different times in each of the phases caused by the diverse influences.

The times when these will each be displayed in the individual will be under such conditions as when there are similar vibrations to excite any particular influence. For instance: We will suppose that Mercury is receiving a good aspect from Jupiter, by direction, which will give an uplifting tendency to the mind, making the native more cheerful and buoyant, increasing the optimism and the desire to see only the bright side of life—and at the same time there may be an adverse aspect from Saturn, also by direction, and the tendency through this is for the mind to become depressed, to be pessimistic, to worry and to look on the dark side of things.

Now when there are transiting aspects from Jupiter to Mercury, even though unfavorable, they will have the power to awaken the first aspect into action, and thus the native will display that outlook on life indicated by the contact of these two planets. If the aspect of the transit be entirely good, the mind will be unusually clear and lucid and the judgment better than usual. Further, almost any good aspect from the other planets to the place of Mercury or Jupiter, at such a time, would have the power to awaken this good influence, and thus there would be a continual play upon the influence throughout the year.

Now, let us take the other aspect, the evil one to Saturn. The same thing will apply in this case. Every time there is an aspect of Mercury or Saturn to those progressed places, whether good or ill, the tendency will be the same—increased, of course, when the aspect is distinctly evil, and less noticeable in its effects when the aspects are good. And, in like case, whenever there is an adverse aspect of any of the other planets to these places, they will tend to awaken the same tendencies according to the strength of the aspects and the nature of the planet. As a total result we will find that the person with these varied influences playing upon him would be what is generally termed very temperamental.

This will be very marked if Mercury is afflicted at the time of birth, or if Gemini or Virgo is rising in the nativity, for such people will be more easily affected by these influences, since they are mentally and nervously sensitive and respond more readily to operating influences of Mercury. But the more stable type of persons, particularly those with fixed signs rising, or the ruler or Mercury in a fixed sign, will be less readily moved by such progressed influences and the results will therefore be much less marked.

It is therefore necessary to study the basic character of the native before you can possibly judge how he will respond to the influences that will play upon him from time to time. Aspects to Mercury should be considered in almost all cases as more important than any other, especially where Mercury is dominant, for it is thought and the result of influences upon the mind that rules all voluntary actions. At this time we are not speaking of the conditions which come to a person through no apparent act of his own and which take on the appearance of fate.

It would be impossible to take the space to cite every possible influence and combination of influences that could occur with Mercury, but sufficient has been said to illustrate the point, and any sincere, hard-working student will be able to work out the rest for himself. One more illustration, however, will not be amiss.

In Plate I Virgo is rising upon the ascendant and this gives Mercury as the ruler of the horoscope. In due course Scorpio became the progressed ascendant and Saturn, by transit, crossed this point. By direction Mercury had just passed a square of the radical Saturn, and while Saturn was in this progressed ascendant he squared the radical Mercury and this produced a mental depression. Thus things which were the phantom of his own brain became very real to him and made him think that people in general were very much against him. Also, it brought strong influences to bear in which he may have been involved in affairs which could have placed him in a very awkward position in connection with writings, speech and agreements had he not, through much experience, been exceedingly cautious. The conditions were accentuated by Uranus transiting in opposition to the radical ascendant and so all things of a Mercurial nature were stirred into action. Had it not been for the many good influences which were operating at the same time, the effects could have been very serious and far-reaching. In this chart the influences of Mars usually act for good, for you will notice Mars has none but good aspects (a trine to the Moon and sextile to Saturn) and is a very much needed force in such a chart, where otherwise the vital forces are somewhat lacking. Some might say that the quincunx (150 degrees) to the ascendant was an affliction, but in this case it is not really so, for it serves to give vitality and resistance to the physical body, which is what the ascendant represents. It was probably the position of Mars at the time of this last incident, he being angular, that saved the native from a nervous breakdown.

In regard to the power of the planets, the Sun comes next, though, taken as a whole and regarded from a different standpoint, the Sun is considered the most important of all, since whatever he brings strikes at the very heart of the individual. The Sun has the power to completely dominate a situation or condition, just as the Leo person seems to have the power, or the desire, or both, to rule all those with whom he comes in contact. His desire is to be the center of attraction, that all others shall be subject to his spell and do him homage. Therefore when the Sun's aspects are good, everything is flourishing, for the king is in good humor, and no other influences have the power to dominate the situation, even though they may dampen it to some extent. And, when the aspects of the Sun are evil, there is need for a sequence of other good vibrations through the other planets to counteract the effects to any appreciable extent. The Sun always works towards nobility of character and there is a lack of "smallness" in all

to which he pertains. He inclines to greater egotism for expansion of self, for the development of the individuality and
for upliftment into more important spheres. When afflicted,
the tendency will be towards pompousness, superiority and
absorption in self.

The Moon is changeable in nature and rules the personality
and astral spheres. The Sun rules in a fixed and stable manner, while the Moon is changeable and restless. They are the
opposite one of the other, and a good interchange of these two
in a chart makes for balance and poise.

Venus has power over all things that have to do with the
feelings and emotions. She provides the outlet for the affections and gives us a desire for beauty, luxury, friends, pleasures
and so forth, depending upon the planet with which she is connected. With Mercury, there is a love of mental pursuits and
art; with Neptune, a love of the esthetic and of the stage, of
odors, and all things pertaining to the sensuous. With Uranus,
a love of romance, and the unusual and unconventional, as
well as of curious and ancient things. With Mars, there is a
love of fight and battle and for things which stand for progress and for dominance in the world of feeling. Venus with
Saturn tends towards the quieter things, deeper and more constant. Those who have Venus with Saturn are more reserved
in their affections, truer and more loyal and unchanging.
While Venus with Jupiter gives the opposite, greater expansion in friendships, in life, in social affairs and in all the
things that Jupiter represents.

Mars is the fighter. He stands ready to take the world and
all that is in it. There is not much of real selfishness in his
vibrations. The whole world seems to him to be for action
and accomplishment, with little love for the thing when once
it is attained, but ever longing to push forward and accomplish something more. It should be borne in mind that
Mars stands for progression and action and will express
himself in this manner according to the nature of the planet
or sign with which he is associated. Here is an example:
If Mars is associated with Uranus, there will be revolutionary tendencies, a desire to accomplish the unusual, to explore
and to seek new fields. But if he is connected with Saturn,
there will be less rush and impulse and an interest in plan-

ning for things further afield that are neither revolutionary nor reactionary, but tending more to steady and improve the present conditions. Also he will show greater ability to work out all problems with tact and diplomacy.

Jupiter brings to us our greatest blessings, unasked and unsought. When he is ready he brings us good things and all we have to do is to be ready to take them when they come. With Mars it is different. He demands energy and enterprise, and unless we act and are up and doing, the things that Mars promises will not come but will lie dormant and untouched.

Saturn stands alone in regard to the manner of his influence. He is slow and deliberate. He brings to us those things which are our fate, the things over which we have no control. It is impossible to override the effects of Saturn, for it is just like hitting against a stone wall. He sets up barriers and obstacles to delay us, requires us to learn from what we have, and when we are ready for the next lesson, he releases us and on we go.

The mission of Uranus is to break up old conditions. He is progressive and constructive, and the reason that most of us feel that his influences are evil is because we respond more to the influence of Saturn than Uranus, for we incline to ruts, clinging to the old things, preferring to hold on to what we have rather than to try anything new, and thus we find it hard when Uranus comes into our lives and shakes us out of our present conditions without consulting us. And yet, who is there among us who does not feel that it is better so, when once the change has been made, or ever regrets that he is not going along in the same old way?

Neptune's actions are less definite. In all ways, however, he makes us more sensitive. He brings to us the experiences which affect our emotional nature and works more upon the astral body than the physical. It is thus that he gets at the root of things and therefore all the results are more subtle and difficult to control from this plane. Those who are easily swayed and influenced through their emotions have more difficulty in working through the influences of Neptune. For, acting as he does, upon the very center of the nervous system, he may disrupt the whole physical organism if response is not harmonious.

CHAPTER 5.

PROGRESSION OF PLANETS THROUGH THE SIGNS.

When a planet progresses into a cardinal sign some kind of a change usually takes place, according to the nature of the planet, the sign and the house. There will be some variation in the manner of living, and affairs generally will materialize into more definite action. When planets progress into fixed signs, conditions become more settled and firmly established, whether applying to health, sickness, wealth, poverty or any other condition in which we may have become involved.

Planets entering into the mutable signs make their influences felt more on the mental plane and usually bring about some kind of a change in thoughts, ideas and aspirations. Much depends upon the nature of the planet. For instance, if the planet were Mars, there would be a mental quickening and activity; if Venus, the thoughts would turn to love, beauty and pleasures, even though there were no hope of obtaining these things. But it is the Sun and Moon which have the most decided effects when entering new signs, the Sun having more influence than the Moon.

When a planet is coming towards the end of a sign its influence is not so potent and indicates the results are rather more towards reaping than sowing. The reverse applies to the planets just entering new signs, as we have shown. In the latter case the native tends to take on new characteristics and develop new qualities. We often hear of persons saying that they used to prefer this kind of food or that for their diet and now never touch it; or that they used to read a great deal, or walk, or engage in music, and now have completely changed their habits. Or they may have been engaged in certain kinds of work and now have changed to something entirely different. Or it may be that their lives used to be quiet and humdrum and now things have altered so that they have no leisure moments at all. All these things are the results of the planets entering new signs, or new signs coming to the angles, the eastern angle being the most susceptible.

(36)

THE SUN.

The Sun progressing out of one sign to another has more effect upon the character of a person than has any other influence and the effect is more decided upon those who respond to their Progressed Charts and are progressing inwardly than upon those who are less responsive to new influences.

Sun in Aries.

At this time there will be new ideas, aims and ambitions, renewed energy and vigor, all the enthusiasm and joy of new enterprises and, with the joy of accomplishment still with him, at the ending of the one cycle, the mind will reach away ahead to the next goal and only with the Sun's progress into the fixed sign Taurus once again will the mind be brought back to earth and to practical accomplishment. Surely it is not hard to see the great scheme of evolution in all this.

There are times when the influence of the Sun is not so strong as that of the planets, the former being weakened either by sign or position, while one or more of the planets may be elevated by sign or position and resulting aspects will thus have more power to affect the Progressed Chart. It would take too much space to go into all the combinations of the planets in the different signs, but a few illustrations will give the principles and the student may work the rest out for himself.

If Mercury were in Scorpio at the time of birth, the mental processes would not be so rapid as if Mercury were in a cardinal or mutable sign, but there would be finer perception, keen penetration and thoroughness in all thought and action. But when Mercury passes into Sagittarius in the Progressed Chart, there should come an expansion and elevation of thought and a greater intuition, so that the whole consciousness may be raised to a higher level. Venus, the love planet, in Leo in a nativity, tends to give greater love of self, strong emotions and passions, love of luxury and so forth, but progressing into Virgo would cause the native to show signs of change and there would be a gradual purifying in sex matters, a growing seriousness and a greater love for humanity and desire for service. All, of course, depending upon how much the native is able to respond to the progression.

To those who are of a very low grade the new influences would work out in the way of depriving them of those things upon which their hearts are set. Mars in Sagittarius at the time of birth gives a venturesome nature, ever ready to take a chance and too often rash and impulsive, but when Mars progresses into Capricorn there is then a great change, for Mars is nowhere so well placed as in this sign and there will be steadiness added to natural courage and the character will thus be deepened and intensified and will finally lose all tendency to rashness and impulse.

Sun in Taurus.

Those who have the Sun in Aries in their Natal Chart find that when he passes into Taurus they have lost something of their impulsiveness and enthusiasm, but are growing to be more reliable and stable both in their thoughts and actions, and there is a greater earnestness of purpose in all that they undertake. They do not desire to do so much, but stick closer to whatever they may be engaged upon. They may develop a greater fondness for food, sweets and luxuries, and in many ways show change and reform according to the amount of knowledge they have gained while the Sun was in Aries. The object of this, of course, is the garnering of all that is desirable in a sign and the discarding of all that is not good for the permanent use of the soul. This applies to the progress of the Sun and all the planets through all of the signs. The Sun in Aries brings change, activity and prominence, but when the Sun enters Taurus the life becomes less changeable and less eventful and those events which do occur have a more lasting effect and go deeper into the consciousness.

Sun in Gemini.

The Sun passing into Gemini will make the native more perceptive and critical, as well as more versatile and intellectual, and tend to develop the general characteristics of that sign, retaining, of course, all that he has gained by his progress through the other signs, and adding more to his character as he experiences new influences.

Sun in Cancer.

The Sun progressing into Cancer, which is his own negative sign, is not so good, and his passage through this sign will bring greater conflicts. The chances are that he will find it difficult to get the best out of the experiences he will have to undergo. The individual does not have the same free expression in this sign, as may be readily understood, since Cancer is the vehicle for the personality, and not the individuality, so that the conditions are not harmonious for his expression. It does, however, tend to bring out a greater love of home and domestic affairs. There will be opportunities for developing the love nature and the maternal instincts, but the vibrations incline one too much to introspection and self-consideration. The intellectual side will be less in evidence; the interest and activities centering more on the environment and domestic affairs. All events will be applied to the personality, clouding the outlook and warping the judgment. This is especially true when the Sun is in the first decanate. The pitfall of the whole sign is supersensitiveness. The second decanate brings the Mars element into play and this tends to increase the feelings and emotions, while with the third decanate comes the Neptunian influence, which tends towards the subtle and psychic and also to develop the sympathies and understanding.

Sun in Leo.

The passing of the Sun into Leo is of course very good, for being now in his own sign, he feels more at home and in harmony, and thus has more power to express the individuality. There will naturally be more egotism and dominance of character, and with those who are not able to express a great deal of their higher nature, there will be a greater love of display and power. But for the ones who are on the upward path there will shine forth a radiance such as the Sun himself gives forth, and the individual will stand before the world in light and glory. The first decanate of this sign is the best, but with Jupiter as co-ruler of the second decanate there will be the opportunity to attain a more philosophical attitude towards life and an increased interest in all the higher sciences and philosophies. The last decanate will be the most difficult to work through, for the Mars element being too strong, the forces will tend to cause assertiveness and impulsiveness, and self-control will be more difficult to maintain.

Sun in Virgo.

With the Sun coming into the mutable sign of Virgo there will be less vitality of the body, and more of the mind. The native will take a more industrious and conscientious attitude towards his duties, but will have less strength and energy to work with than while the Sun was still in Leo. He will have fewer opportunities on the material plane, but will be able to develop a finer mentality, become more observant and perceptive, and, with the interests centering more and more upon detail and perfection, he will steadily progress towards his goal.

Sun in Libra.

The Sun progressing into Libra brings a new cycle, and the experiences will now be more in connection with other people. Libra itself represents the completement, in some other person, or persons, of oneself, and the whole of the second half of the circle represents this other person to some extent, and the native's relation to him. Thus, the Sun entering Libra will frequently bring about marriage and always indicates closer companionship with others in many ways that have not been experienced before.

The opportunities thus afforded for developing the faculty of cooperation and agreeableness are great, and learned in the right way make an invaluable asset for continuing the journey through the rest of the signs. It is rarely, of course, if ever, that we are able to show all that we have learned while the Sun has been passing through the various signs. Yet that

knowledge is never lost, and we pick it up again and demonstrate it whenever the vibrations are harmonious with that
particular quality. We have the opportunity, also, to get a
better sense of values when the Sun is in Libra; to develop a
keener sense of justice, and to obtain a better balance in every
way, though the unprogressive will be inclined to lean too
much on other people, to be too dependent, losing to some
extent their own initiative and make greater demands all the
time upon those with whom their lives are interwoven.

Sun in Scorpio.

There is quite a difference in the natural characteristics of
Libra and the following sign, Scorpio. When the Sun enters
this latter sign the native becomes more positive and more
in earnest in everything he undertakes. The developed soul
working through this sign will be more courageous and daunt-
less, ready to sacrifice anything to accomplish that which he
has set himself to do, and, instead of depending and relying
too much upon other people, will take upon himself all the
burden and responsibilities entailed in the enterprise. He will
find himself becoming more psychic and interested in occult
subjects and will begin to look upon life and death in a new
way altogether. The less progressive tend, under this influence, to become more callous, to be less considerate of others
and to desire to bend them to their will and ambitions.

The Sun is the life-giver and he immediately begins to awaken
all the possibilities that are contained in each of the signs as
he enters them, bringing the latent faculties into use, satisfactorily or otherwise, according to the natural inclinations
of the individual and the manner in which the rays descend
upon the sign. By that we mean that the Sun helps himself,
so to speak, from the other planets, and if the line of contact
(in other words, the aspects that are made from any given
sign) is harmonious he will be able to work through that sign
successfully, giving the best opportunities during his sojourn
there, but if his relation with the other planets is inharmonious, the possibilities of the sign cannot be brought out to the
best advantage. Let us suppose that the Sun, either at birth

or by progression, makes a square to Mars, and enters the sign of Scorpio, which is ruled by Mars, we will find that the result will be an accentuation of the adverse aspect and it will not be easy for the native to make as good use of the possibilities of the sign as he could if the aspect were a benefic one.

Sun in Sagittarius.

The Sun progressing into the fortunate and philosophical sign of Sagittarius rarely fails to improve the whole nature and character. This sign, ruled by the great benefic, Jupiter, and belonging to the house of the higher mind, brings opportunities for development in all the higher lines of thought and should enable one to take long flights of imagination and to enter into lines of thought and consciousness of which he has never before been aware. The possibilities here are great, even for material success, for speculation, for travel and for dealings with, or for, foreign countries.

Sun in Capricorn.

From this sign the Sun enters Capricorn, the sign that belongs to business, profession and public affairs, and this position brings better chances for some publicity and prominence, or an opportunity to assume new responsibilities, either in ordinary business affairs or in those that concern the general public, and if the rest of the chart agrees, a period will be entered into when there will be a rise both in social and professional standing, and an increase in honor and importance.

It is possible for the Sun to be in as many as four different signs during any normal span of life, and the influence of the Sun, by progression, into any sign, must be considered with its radical position and the possibilities and potentialities of the latter. For an example we will take one who has the Sun in Virgo in the Natal Chart with the Sun progressing into Libra. This would give the natural industrious and practical quality of Virgo to work through, and with, other people and would give an opportunity to show real service, but with the Sun arriving in the powerful sign of Scorpio there would be a clashing of forces with the sensitive, nervous temperament of Virgo, making the native increasingly irritable and exacting.

But, if the Sun were in the last decanate of Libra in the nativity, and then progressed into Scorpio, the natural gentleness and cooperation of Libra would remain and there would be a strengthening of the weak side of Libra, adding a sense of responsibility and independence, so that the balance should be a very good one, and the development considerable. It would certainly be much easier than the progress would be from Virgo, through Libra to Scorpio, from a sensitive, mutable sign to the positive and domineering one.

When the Sun enters Sagittarius, the whole tendency of thought and aspiration will be elevated. Those qualities that fit men to become successful lawyers and judges will be developed. These qualities, inherent in Libra, develop more fully while the Sun passes through Sagittarius, during that time often giving him opportunity of establishing himself in such a manner that when the Sun passes from Sagittarius into the Cardinal sign of Capricorn, which tends to prominence, the native attains some fame.

The student must understand that though the Sun in a Cardinal sign at birth indicates prominence, this may not be attained until the Sun enters the next Cardinal sign, because if at birth the Sun is not in an early degree, he will have passed from that sign before the native has time to establish himself.

Progress is likely to be slower while the Sun is in Capricorn because of the retarding influence of the ruler Saturn. But progress will be sure, and for those who are far-seeing and persevering there is great promise. This sign deals with political economy and the great issues of the public and the scope is very great for those who have the necessary abilities and long vision.

Sun in Aquarius.

The passing of the Sun from Capricorn to Aquarius rarely fails to make a change in the life and temperament of the individual. The change of life is usually due to a change of thought, for everything is seen from a different standpoint.

From publicity and contact with the world in a more selfish manner, so to speak, where personal gain and honor are sought, through the Capricorn influence, we get to the more universal aspect, with an increasing desire to work for humanity as a whole. The Sun, having now passed through Capricorn, bringing worldly honor and position, the native is due to be weary of such things and will have learned in the meantime of the needs of the "Great Orphan, Humanity," and will now have more desire to work in that direction without honor or glory for himself. When this point is reached the individual is nearing the end of the cycle, the goal is almost attained, and the mission of that incarnation, or series of incarnations, will be accomplished. The Sun in Aquarius brings the desire to start, or to join, brotherhoods and those organizations which are formed solely for philanthropic purposes. Life will now probably lack the prominence and public work of the previous sign, but much work may be accomplished and an inner progress made, greater than will be visible on the surface. The imagination will be increased, so also the aspiration, and many of the faculties that belong to the airy signs in general.

Sun in Pisces.

We now come to the last, and greatest, of all the signs, Pisces. The ultimate possibilities of this sign are so far removed from the ordinary individual that he cannot even surmise them, let alone attain to them. They are entirely spiritual and very exalted. But there is opportunity for progress for each individual in some direction made chiefly through self-denial and sacrifice, not willingly (excepting in rare cases) but forced upon the individual and brought about by the stored-up karma of past incarnations. It becomes a purifying process, but is hard to bear and many sad events occur, or the native is brought into contact with those who have much sorrow and through whom he may have to learn many lessons. So with those whose charts are afflicted, the Sun in this sign will be felt intensely, but if, as should be, after the Sun has passed through Aquarius, the aims and aspirations have been purified, the end of the cycle will bring some triumph and a readiness to begin the new cycle of conditions and experiences when the Sun again passes into Aries, the first sign of the Zodiac.

THE MOON.

The Moon should be considered especially, both as to sign and house, for she plays a very important part in the Progressed Horoscope. The aspects of the Sun, by progression, are like the hour hands on a clock. They are the most important, but, at the same time, the most general. The Moon corresponds to the minute hand, while the transits would represent the seconds, and it is these which bring events to the particular moment of action. The Moon moves so quickly that she progresses through the entire cycle in 28 years. This means that a new sign is entered approximately every two and a half years. The influence of the Moon in each sign is modified by the sign she is in at the time of birth and, of course, with the aspects that she makes at that time. The delineation of the Progressed Horoscope in combination with the nativity must rest with the intuition and experience of each student, but below are given the influences of the Moon in the signs, in a general way.

Moon in Aries.

The Moon progressing into Aries will cause the mind to work quicker and be more active. While the Moon is in this sign the native will be more impulsive than usual, will talk and act more quickly and be less patient, but more enterprising. Thus, if we found, in the Progressed Chart, that the Sun had come to a good aspect with Jupiter and the Moon had entered Aries, he would have the necessary impetus and enterprise to push his affairs and to make the most of the good solar vibrations, for, while all good aspects of the Sun and Jupiter will bring things unlooked for and unasked, they may remain unnoticed and unused if we do not know how to take and use them. The saying, "God helps them who help themselves," is very true, and thus it is when the Moon is in the sign, or connected with a planet, that will give the necessary push and enterprise, that the native may make the most use of those things which time and tide are bringing to him. But, with the Moon in Aries, there will be a tendency to head-aches, some sudden sickness or rushes of blood to the head, feverishness or giddiness, depending upon the aspects that the Moon may make. In her passage through all the signs, the Moon is liable to affect that part of the body and bring that type of disease that is signified by that sign, always depend-ing, of course, upon her own aspects or those of the transit-ing planets, for the excitement of those complaints.

Moon in Taurus.

With the Moon in Taurus the mind will work more slowly and deliberately. The native will feel that he must be more conservative, must change his methods and make provision for the proverbial rainy day. He will begin to realize, through the mistakes he probably made while the Moon was in Aries, that it is poor policy to act without thought, and will thus begin to make a practice of sleeping on his plans before acting. If the reaction, in the changing from the one sign to the other, is great, there might be a slump and a change into laziness and inaction. Home will look good to him now, and he will probably resolve to stay in it more, do some entertaining and pay off many obligations that have been accumulating during the previous two or three years, while the Moon was passing through Aries, and thus he enters into a new field of action.

Moon in Gemini.

The Moon in Gemini will bring another change. Talents hitherto dormant will now come to the surface. The mind will again become active, but not in the same way as when the Moon was in Aries. The native will be more thoughtful, perceptive and studious and also more critical and sensitive. More writing and study will be done and all things that have to do with correspondence, signing of papers, selling, buying and so forth, will occupy time and thought. Relatives will play a more important part, there will be changes and short journeys and the native will, in general, be more restless and unsettled.

Moon in Cancer.

The Moon passing into Cancer will bring the affairs of the home into consideration. There will be moves and changes in this connection and the native will be anxious to improve and to plan for extensions in the home environment.

Moon in Leo.

With the Moon in Leo amusements are likely to absorb the mind. It must be remembered that the Moon absorbs and expresses those qualities that any sign contains and uses them for personal benefits and additions only, since the Moon is purely personal. That is why it is her aspects which cause the precipitation of action upon this personal plane. The Moon in Leo will also accentuate the feelings and emotions, bring some love affairs into the life and also some connections with children or young people.

Moon in Virgo.

When the Moon enters Virgo there is greater attention paid to hygiene, health and diet. The vitality is lowered and there will not be the same flow of circulation. It may now be necessary to work more for others and probably receive less consideration and recognition; and the chances are that those in employment may make changes for better or worse, according to the nature of the aspects that the Moon may make while in this sign.

Moon in Libra.

When the Moon enters Libra it is probable that connection will be made with some other person or persons which will prove of distinct benefit, and this will make affairs flow along a somewhat different channel. Conditions will be improved and the native's field of activity will be enlarged.

Moon in Scorpio.

The Moon is not comfortable in Scorpio and the general tendency, especially in a woman's chart, is toward poor health and general debility. Infectious diseases are more easily contracted when the Moon is in Scorpio. The temper will not be so serene, there will be more passion and less hold on the emotions.

Moon in Sagittarius.

The Moon entering Sagittarius should bring a distinct improvement. As in the case with all planets when they enter this sign or the house to which it naturally belongs, there is a general tendency towards upliftment both in thought and ideals. With the Moon in this sign, if the nativity promises it, there will be some travel, or more outdoor activities, and the body will be generally more active and inclined to sports and exercise.

Moon in Capricorn.

The Moon in Capricorn brings changes in business or profession, not necessarily detrimental, and often to the honor and advantage of the native. With good aspects it makes for progress and benefits through public offices or through the employer, and while the Moon is not so strong in this sign of her fall, yet it tends towards carefulness in the fulfillment of one's duty, thoughtfulness and gain through one's own merit and hard work.

Moon in Aquarius.

When the Moon passes into Aquarius the mind becomes more expansive and the whole trend of thought and action broadens. There will be closer and better contact with friends, resulting in joining some society and taking greater interest in charities and outside affairs.

Moon in Pisces.

And, lastly, the Moon in Pisces will probably bring the native in contact with sorrow and trouble and with those who are confined in hospitals and institutions, and if the native's own health is endangered at this time, it is more than likely he will have to go to a hospital or be closely confined to his own home for a time. There may be some occult or astral experiences, contact with other planes than the material, and some connections with the water or with those places that are situated by the ocean.

CHAPTER 6.

PROGRESSED ASCENDANT.

Each sign is divided into three main divisions of ten degrees each and these are called decanates. The decanates in which planets or angles fall have considerable importance, especially in the Progressed Chart. The effect of either of these in any decanate is similar to its conjunction with the ruler of such decanate. The ruler of any decanate, rising to the ascendant in the Progressed Chart, has a great deal of influence over the whole life, for the time being, particularly if that ruler should make any strong aspects at that time, or if the planet should be strong in the Natal Chart. Each decanate has a ruler, which is the planet belonging to the next sign under the same element in the order in which they follow one another, as will be seen in the table below.

Sign	*Aries*	*Taurus*	*Gemini*	*Cancer*
	(Fire)	(Earth)	(Air)	(Water)
Ruler first decanate...	Mars	Venus	Mercury	Moon
Ruler second decanate	Sun	Mercury	Venus	Mars
Ruler third decanate..	Jupiter	Saturn	Uranus	Neptune
Sign	*Leo*	*Virgo*	*Libra*	*Scorpio*
Ruler first decanate...	Sun	Mercury	Venus	Mars
Ruler second decanate	Jupiter	Saturn	Uranus	Neptune
Ruler third decanate..	Mars	Venus .	Mercury	Moon
Sign	*Sagittarius*	*Capricorn*	*Aquarius*	*Pisces*
Ruler first decanate...	Jupiter	Saturn	Uranus	Neptune
Ruler second decanate	Mars	Venus	Mercury	Moon
Ruler third decanate..	Sun	Mercury	Venus	Mars

Thus it will be seen that the ruler of the sign as a whole rules entirely the first decanate and is followed by the ruler of the next sign of the same element, and the third by the ruler of the remaining sign of that trio.

The signs are divided, also, into twelve parts. These divisions are made in different ways, but the one given here is the old Hindu method, which seems to be the most reasonable and logical, being based on exact mathematical division. As the following table shows, the signs are divided into twelve equal parts of 2½ degrees each, and the ruler of each division is the ruler of the sign which is next in sequence.

Sign	1 2½	2 5	3 7½	4 10	5 12½	6 15	7 17½	8 20	9 22½	10 25	11 27½	12 30
Aries	♂	♀	☿	☽	☉	☿	♀	♂	♃	♄	♅	♆
Taurus	♀	☿	☽	☉	☿	♀	♂	♃	♄	♅	♆	♂
Gemini	☿	☽	☉	☿	♀	♂	♃	♄	♅	♆	♂	♀
Cancer	☽	☉	☿	♀	♂	♃	♄	♅	♆	♂	♀	☿
Leo	☉	☿	♀	♂	♃	♄	♅	♆	♂	♀	☿	☽
Virgo	☿	♀	♂	♃	♄	♅	♆	♂	♀	☿	☽	☉
Libra	♀	♂	♃	♄	♅	♆	♂	♀	☿	☽	☉	☿
Scorpio	♂	♃	♄	♅	♆	♂	♀	☿	☽	☉	☿	♀
Sagittarius ...	♃	♄	♅	♆	♂	♀	☿	☽	☉	☿	♀	♂
Capricorn	♄	♅	♆	♂	♀	☿	☽	☉	☿	♀	♂	♃
Aquarius	♅	♆	♂	♀	☿	☽	☉	☿	♀	♂	♃	♄
Pisces	♆	♂	♀	☿	☽	☉	☿	♀	♂	♃	♄	♅

It is not so easy to make the same use of these divisions as it is of the decanates, as they represent finer points in delineation, but they are well worth study by the student and will reveal many things that would otherwise be obscure, and will many times show the reason for events that cannot be found any other way. Particular note should be made of the Sun as he progresses into these divisions through any given sign and also to the progressed ascendant and midheaven. As an instance, take Aries. All of this sign contains a martial influence, particularly the first decanate, and, still more particularly, the first two and a half degrees. The effect of the Sun in these first degrees would be almost exactly the same as though he were conjunct Mars. The native will show a great increase of energy and ambition, will probably be too active and rash and anxious to push forward in all the things in which he is interested. But, as the Sun passes into the degrees ruled by Venus, he will immediately begin to feel some of that planet's influence and this should soften the effect of the Mars vibration, thus making him less impulsive and more practical, though more amorous. And so on, through all the degrees and decanates. It is not possible for the student to do anything with this part of the astrological synthesis unless he thoroughly understands the nature and effects of the planets and the signs.

This brings us to the point where we must discuss what are called primary directions. That is, the influence of the signs, as they rise, bringing a new degree to the ascendant approximately every year, depending upon the latitude in which the native was born. As has already been explained, the Progressed Horoscope is erected on the plan of a day representing a year. Every four minutes of time brings a new degree to the ascendant throughout each day and a new sign approximately every two hours. This is due to the rotation of the Earth upon its own axis, and as this takes almost exactly four minutes less than twenty-four hours, it is easy to see that she will be four minutes ahead of time each succeeding day. So the relation of any given time would show four minutes of space ahead of her position the day before, which in turn represents one degree of longitude and would thus show another degree of the same sign that was rising at that time on the previous day. This progression, then, as the years go by, will draw the planets away from the position they were in, in the Natal Chart, and pull them around to different parts of the circle as related to their natal positions.

This briefly is what is known as Primary Directions. They are the only directions based on the actual rotation of the earth. Other directions are symbolic, though not less potent, especially those with which this treatise mostly deals—Secondary Directions—which to the author seem more powerful than Primary Directions.

Keeping in mind the object of this treatise: to simplify the Progressed Horoscope—because Primary Directions, with the exception of the Progressed Ascendant, involve considerable mathematical calculations—no other Primary Directions but the Progressed Ascendant will be considered herein.

We will not, in this work, take the time or space to give the influence of the twelve divisions of each sign as they rise, but will confine ourselves to the decanates.

(*Note.*—It must be remembered that, while this is written for application of the progressed ascendant, it will apply, to a greater or lesser extent, when any of the other cusps, or any of the planets, arrive at these decanates. The tendencies will have to be combined with the nature of the house or the planet, and also the general tendencies of those planets, and the rulers of the decanate, in the Natal and Progressed Charts. This is, of course, a complicated procedure and it is best, for those who have not had much experience, to leave this section alone for the time being.)

Aries.

First Decanate; ruler, Mars.—The progression of this sign to the ascendant will have much effect upon the mind and quicken its action in every way. There will be increased ambition and a greater desire to lead and to rule. The force and energy which this influence brings helps the native to become more prominent and to secure some kind of honor or a more important position. He will be keener and more alive in every way, ready to take charge of things, to attempt more than he has time and strength for, and will take a keen interest in many things that had no attraction for him before. This is mainly because he will now be looking for an outlet for the increase of energy, both mental and physical, that this new sign and decanate will bring to him. This decanate is a very important one, because it is the start of a new cycle, the end of which will largely depend on the manner and the direction in which the native uses his increased energy.

Second Decanate; rulers, Mars and the Sun.—The combination here is good, for the Sun tends to elevate all that comes within his sphere of influence. There will be the same energy and desire for action, but the turn of mind will be towards nobler and better things and the progress of the earnest person will be great. It will bring affairs of the fifth house more definitely to the fore. That is, there will be greater interest in speculation and in all kinds of amusements. To those who are of the age and inclination there will be love affairs, and to others a greater interest in, or contact with, children. This is a splendid combination of the fiery signs and should send the aspirations towards higher things, quicken the emotions and call out all the sympathies of the heart.

Third Decanate; rulers, Mars and Jupiter.—This combination is hardly so good, for whenever Mars and Jupiter come together there is a lack of steadfastness and a greater tendency towards impulse, extravagance and expenditures. On the higher planes it is very good, for impulse and expansion here are needed and thus there can be brought about a loftier spirit, a daring for truth, a desire to go deeper into all fields of knowledge and usually a progressive spirit that is very elevating. On the lower planes it is not so good, for there will be a lack of caution, the possibility of becoming entangled in litigation and many disputes or disagreements if the native is at all inclined that way.

Taurus.

First Decanate; ruler, Venus.—Since Taurus rules the second house, which is the house of money, this new sign coming to the ascendant will bring financial matters more to the fore. The native will become more fixed, more practical and more settled. There will be less ambition, but more perseverance and, therefore, a better chance for accomplishment or for reaching any set goal. If the spiritual tendencies coming from the previous sign, and particularly the last decanate, have been cultivated, the influences from this new sign will be sufficient to make them workable. If Venus is well aspected, and other things agree, there will be prosperity and financial benefits.

Second Decanate; rulers, Venus and Mercury.—Now the intellect will take on a new activity, for the influence of Mercury always tends to awaken the mental faculties to still greater activity. This decanate will make a person more talkative, more inclined to social pleasures and likely to contact those who are musical and fun-loving. All the natural functions of Mercury will show themselves to some extent, such as in matters of the third and sixth houses, things that have to do with service, study, letter writing, health, short journeys, etc. While all affairs will still be carried on in a practical manner, at the same time there will be thought and aspiration with it, and so all things will be accomplished with thoroughness and intelligence.

Third Decanate; rulers, Venus and Saturn.—With the Saturnine element coming in here, there will be a steadying and slowing up process in every direction. It will be a good influence, provided Venus and Saturn are favorable in the nativity, for this combination brings constancy, cements friendships and ties and brings permanent satisfaction and results. To those who are able to make the right response there will be a substantial progress and a likelihood of some honor or responsibility that will bring an increase in income. All the time that this sign is rising there will be an effect upon the finances, either to the detriment or the benefit of the subject, according to the nature of the chart as a whole. This rule will apply (according to their natures and to the house to which they naturally belong) to all the signs as they rise upon the ascendant.

Gemini.

First Decanate; ruler, Mercury.—As with the beginning of any new sign there comes to the individual the opportunity to contact a new set of experiences, either physical or mental or both, but, with such a sign as Gemini now rising, it is more likely to be mental than physical, particularly with the first decanate on the ascendant, though, of course, action on any plane will have some effect upon all the other planes, and this specially in regard to these two, physical and mental. There will now be mental activity in all directions; more discrimination will be displayed, and a keener sense of criticism and perception. Things that ordinarily would pass the native by will now be perceived without apparent effort. There will be a general awakening of the intellect, a new desire to study and to learn, and at the same time a mental restlessness that could cause some changes in the life and journeys that would satisfy both the desire for change and knowledge.

Second Decanate; rulers, Mercury and Venus.—This is the same combination that we get in the second decanate of Taurus, with this difference, that the main influence now is the intellectual Mercury instead of the practical financier, Venus, and the Mercurial influence in this case comes through the imaginative, restless sign Gemini, while the Venus influence comes through the balanced and just sign of Libra. This brings opportunity for very great internal progress. There will be new lines of thought entered upon; a balancing up of past events and a mental readjustment of many experiences. In some respects the native's life will be a little easier, for the reason that it is most likely that someone else will come in and carry much of the burden. At any rate, there will be a sharing, and more happiness because of this. On the mental plane there will be clearer sight and vision and a better understanding of values, both in people and in things. There is much more that may be read into all the decanates than is written here, but the student, with study and practice, may fill in these details for himself and translate them according to the radical promises and tendencies.

Third Decanate; rulers, Mercury and Uranus.—This is a strong mental combination. It will bring unusual ideas, new thoughts and methods and an inclination to dig deeper into the mysteries of nature and into all occult subjects. It is a good time for one to take an interest in curios and all things that are antique and unusual. This combination gives great opportunities along all lines of higher thought and sciences. Of course, if the native is not of a very progressive nature, these vibrations will not work to the fullest extent upon him, but he is sure to meet with people who will interest him, to some extent, in these things. Since both these planets rule friends, neighbors and those who are closely related, there will be more activity in this direction than usual, and more dealings and benefits, or injuries, may come through them, according to the promise of the nativity.

Cancer.

First Decanate; ruler, the Moon.—Since Cancer and the Moon both have to do with the home and the mother, the activities will now turn in this direction. There will come a greater longing and interest in the home and in domestic affairs and more of the motherly side of the nature will be developed. Cancer persons are usually extremely sensitive and receptive and very keen in their feelings and emotions; and therefore, when this influence begins to play upon them, it is these tendencies that will be aroused. It must be remembered that every sign has potentially the characteristics of all the others, and likewise that each individual has potentially the characteristics of every other individual, so that this is the explanation of why we respond to all the vibrations of all the signs and planets. If we were not potentially the same, only those vibrations which responded to the rate of vibrations within ourselves would, or could, affect us. We are forced to recognize and accept this great fundamental truth in nature, that we are all made the same, and in consequence are obliged to accept the still greater truth, that we all come from the one Source. Thus is it seen that everyone has something of the great mother instinct within him and such opportunities as the sign representing this, Cancer, coming to the ascendant, or the Sun entering that sign, should be used to the fullest extent in order that our natures may be softened and our love and sympathies extended. A keener interest in occult subjects will also be evident, and the personality should have the opportunity for more educational experiences.

Second Decanate; rulers, the Moon and Mars.—This is the least favorable of the Cancer decanates, for the Moon and Mars are never comfortable in close proximity to one another. There is liable to be a constant spluttering because of the mixture of heat and cold and therefore the experiences will be such as will be very trying to the personality. The opportunities are greater for real development, if the personality can stand up under the strain, for it tends to develop a more subtle nature, a deeper interest in occult matters and more mystical tendencies. But, to the person who is not making any special efforts, the tendency will be to become more passionate and jealous, more secretive and too easily stirred to emotion and anger. There is always some danger of infectious diseases under this influence and it is wise not to risk exposure to them.

Third Decanate; rulers, the Moon and Neptune.—Here we note even more subtle influences and an increase of sensitiveness. The tendency in this case will be the reverse of the second decanate; for where Mars brings activity and passion, Neptune inclines towards negativeness and dispassion, too much receptivity and a negative sensuality. But the possibilities are greater and tend towards a more universal love; to unselfishness, hospitality and compassion. In all cases the watery signs increase the emotions, and it depends upon which plane the individual is working as to what emotions will be brought out and in what manner. The watery signs are also the most occult signs and thus there is the opportunity to develop on the higher planes and to increase the knowledge of mystical things.

Leo.

First Decanate; ruler, the Sun.—This is the positive sign of Cancer, or, rather, Cancer is the negative sign of Leo. The one represents the individuality and the other the personality. The Sun, the ruler of Leo, represents the positive, forceful ego, and the Moon, the ruler of Cancer, the negative, changeable personality, and the latter is dependent almost entirely upon the rising sign for its opportunity and mode of expression. Leo rules the heart and the sentiments, and therefore, when this sign comes to the ascendant, there begins new experiences such as will tend to develop the sympathies, feelings and emotions. There should now be an expansion from personal to individual emotions, which means that there is development and growth. The Moon indicates great selfishness and self-absorption, while the Sun is the reverse, extending his interests and affections to all other egos, himself, however, desiring to be the central figure around which others will revolve. It is only when we come to the great and mighty planet Uranus, having the same qualities, on a much higher plane, as Venus and the Sun, that we get the true love and humanitarian interests that have no selfishness in them. The Sun has the power of radiation and warmth, which he imparts to all who come within his radius, and those who now begin to come into the sphere of this decanate's vibrations develop these faculties, as well as greater vitality, strength and independence. In another phase it brings about love affairs, interest in all things sensational and an increased love of pleasure and amusements.

Second Decanate; rulers, the Sun and Jupiter.—This is a progressive and fortunate influence and one which should raise the tone of the mind to a much higher and more exalted state. Since Jupiter rules the ninth house, the individual should become more philosophical and take a greater interest in all metaphysical subjects. This will be the time to work upon and study such lines, since there is every opportunity for the expansion of the mind, while Jupiter has his benefic force in operation. To those whose nativities are favorable this will be a period that is fortunate for speculation, investments and expansion in business and financial affairs. Long journeys may be taken, especially to foreign lands.

Third Decanate; rulers, the Sun and Mars.—This is, of course, not so fortunate, for the combined vibrations of the Sun and Mars bring too much impulse and assertiveness, though in a well-balanced chart it will tend more towards enterprise, energy and progress. But there is always danger of going to extremes; of overdoing and being overconfident and enthusiastic. In a high-class nativity it can be readily understood that there is great opportunity here for the development of the will and the heart together and the right blending of these two on higher planes will be well-directed thought, will, desire and control.

Virgo.

First Decanate; ruler, Mercury.—Having come through all the preceding signs, the ego is now fitted to serve with the right spirit. Life is intended to work out that way. We pass through the influences of these first signs, starting with energy and ambition in Aries, then practical application through

Taurus, and intellectual conception and use in Gemini; then a development of love, first for one's own family through Cancer, and then for others, when we reach the vibrations of Leo, ending up with willingness to serve and to be out of the limelight. The true Virgo is very retiring and modest, makes the best servant and is willing to attend to details. When we begin the second half of the cycle there is a change, for now everything must be done in company and cooperation with others. With Virgo ends the first stage of the ego's development. He begins now to have more discrimination and thoughtfulness. When this sign rises upon the ascendant there is much less opportunity for free will and action and life takes on more the conditions of "fate" and brings those circumstances and events over which the native has little or no control. There is less vitality, less opportunity, and a sense of being held down to the "grindstone". One is apt to become much more sensitive and nervous and ill health will attend anyone whose chart is weak in this direction.

Second Decanate; rulers, Mercury and Saturn.—The fatalistic conditions will be still more marked with Saturn coming into the influences, but still, with this there comes more patience, more perseverance and a more anxious attention to duty. It should make one a better servant and, since Saturn rules the natural tenth house, could bring some sort of recognition or promotion through such services. Whatever comes will be through the native's own perseverance, industry and ability and he will have the joy of knowing that what he does get is well and rightfully earned.

Third Decanate; rulers, Mercury and Venus.—This is the most benefic of the Virgo influences. Finances will improve, there will be more gayety and pleasures in the life, more friends and more opportunities, which will be mainly through friends or relatives. The mind should be brighter and more at peace and there will be flexibility and ability to study along a wider field. With the advent of the influence of Venus the native will quite possibly be more obstinate and self-willed, but, if he is on the upward path, the natural love which will be called forth by Venus will help him out of this and give him a truer sense of service and justice.

Libra.

First Decanate; ruler, Venus.—Everything will now go easier and conditions will be 'much more pleasant. New people will come into the life and will play an important part therein.· Many people (who are of the right age and condition) marry when the first degrees of this sign touch the horizon. It is a critical period in some respects, because, as we have said, it is the beginning of a new cycle and there will be adjustments to be made and new conditions to be considered. There comes a new sense of order and justice and a different aspect of life, more as though it were viewed from another's standpoint and thus, naturally, a wider field of vision is obtained. If there is no marriage, there may be a partner taken, or someone will enter into the life who has many similar interests and views.

Second Decanate; rulers, Venus and Uranus.—Again we get the strong Saturnine influence coming into the life, but the combination here is quite good, for it has a steadying effect, will make for deeper and truer love and will cement marriage, if such has taken place, into a more satisfactory (even if more matter of fact) and lasting condition. Permanent friendships will be made, though if there are any adverse aspects, there will also be permanent enemies, for Libra naturally belongs to the house that rules open antagonism. It brings very suitable influences for the study of human nature and for character reading, for one is drawn into much closer contact with people.

Third Decanate; rulers, Venus and Mercury.—Here again is the combination of Venus and Mercury, which is always good, especially for the mind, for the reason that it always gives a more cheerful and hopeful outlook and brings joy in the more artistic, and softer, pleasanter phases of life. It is likely that there will be travel during this period of ten years, and connections will be closer between relatives and neighbors. It often brings about marriage or partnership between relatives. In business it will bring benefits through cooperation, and it will either make one more interested in the details or force greater attention to them. It will be a good period for all kinds of literary work to those who are naturally suited to that line.

Scorpio.

First Decanate; ruler, Mars.—There is a decided jump from the soft, pliable Libra to the positive, harsh sign of Scorpio. This will bring greater determination, more force, energy and ambition and will thus aid in making manifest all the possibilities that Libra may have brought to life. In the undeveloped it will bring out all the evil side of Scorpio, giving a desire for power, for dominion over others, for sarcasm and secrecy. But to those who are really striving, it will add interest in occult subjects, will bring new experiences in that line and some unusual dreams and visions.

Second Decanate; rulers, Mars and Neptune.—Again we have a combination that is volcanic. There is always danger of eruptions in such a force as comes from the meeting of these two planets, and during the period that this decanate is rising upon the ascendant the native will need to be quite careful and thoughtful in all his actions. Since Scorpio rules the house of death, any evil influences bearing upon the cusp of this progressed ascendant will be likely to bring about a death or some adverse condition in connection with death. Many regrettable events can be brought about while this influence is in operation if the native acts precipitately or runs into needless expense or extravagances. Mars and Jupiter together nearly always cause a waste or leakage, but usually this is under one's own control and may be avoided by discreet and careful action.

Third Decanate; rulers, Mars and the Moon.—Mars does not harmonize with any other planet very well, as is the case with the Mars people; not that they are not admirable in their way, but they are not group-workers and cannot bear to slow down their pace to that of others or to give up or try to blend their own plans with those of others. Thus we find that Mars and the Moon together bring a good deal of clashing; they will "spit fire", as it were, and there will be continual friction. The influence of this decanate rising will cause the native to be more readily excited, will make him more selfish, and because the Moon rules the home, there will be danger of trouble in that direction, if the proper control and discretion is not used. Caution must be the watchword or very trying conditions will result. Excitement, anger and impulse should be checked at once and nothing should be done that is likely to cause overstimulation, either mentally or physically.

Sagittarius.

First Decanate; ruler, Jupiter.—Now we come to a much more fortunate set of vibrations. This is the sign that rules the higher mind, and the ruler, Jupiter, is the great benefic, so that not only will there be a mental uplift, but also good fortune on the material plane. There are many times, however, when it is not possible to have both material and spiritual benefits and we have to choose which of the two we most desire. However, all the time that this sign is upon the ascendant there is a general tendency towards improved conditions and many doors are open that have been sealed before. There is more buoyancy in the air; more faith and hope, and there comes that inner feeling that all will be well. Now is the time when philosophical studies should be taken up, and when knowledge may be gained on higher planes. Whatever there is in the way of natural ability for law or religion may now be developed. Interest in sports will be taken up and all kinds of outdoor exercises, and it is the time when, if the nativity permits it, long journeys will be taken. If they are not taken on the physical plane, long flights of fancy and imagination will take their place.

Second Decanate; rulers, Jupiter and Mars.—Here again we have the clashing of these planets, making this the least favorable of the Sagittarian decanates. Of course, as will readily be seen, this is much more fortunate than the Mars-Jupiter decanate of Scorpio, for the sign itself contains greater possibilities. But still, there will be the same danger of impulse and rashness, of too great an expenditure of energy, time, money or will. There is danger of carelessness and indiscretion, lack of control, insufficient attention to the duties on hand, and too much assertiveness and impulse. Judgment should be tempered with a knowledge of the nature of the vibrations now playing upon the personality, and in that way much danger and adversity will be avoided. All such statements as this apply, of course, to those in whom such tendencies naturally lie. To those who are inclined to be overcautious and conservative, such an influence as is brought about by this decanate will more likely serve as a stimulant and benefic force for renewed action, interest and enthusiasm.

Third Decanate; rulers, Jupiter and the Sun.—This is very much more fortunate and will bring many blessings to the native that have been withheld up to this time. There is some tendency to extremes, either of emotion or in other ways, and for that reason there should be some care used in financial matters, and also in dealing with people generally. But to the ordinarily thoughtful person this will be an exceedingly good influence for progress. It is under such an influence as this, however, that that which has already been spoken of (the choosing between the material and spiritual benefits) may be brought up to the native. The Sun rules the house of speculations and investments and Jupiter is so expansive in his actions and desires that, if the attention and mind of the native are once placed in this direction, it is probable that it will carry him away completely and whatever gains he might derive from this direction will be at the sacrifice of the greater knowledge and progress. One can understand these truths only as he dwells more and more upon the nature of the signs, houses and planets and gets a vision of the effects of these various combinations.

Capricorn.

First Decanate; ruler, Saturn.—Now we come to the business or professional sign. This should bring a greater desire to excel and to come before the public in some work of service. It is the diplomatic and political sign and therefore will tend to bring a new interest in politics to those who are already in that line, and an advance, or increase, of trust and honor. To all those who are working sincerely and industriously along any line it will bring recognition of some kind and a greater ability to handle whatever work and conditions in which they may find themselves.

Second Decanate; rulers, Saturn and Venus.—This is very good because it now brings the Taurus influence, which is also the money influence, and thus all business affairs should be more successful, and money will be freer and more easily acquired. Since the earthy signs are the practical and industrious ones, these traits should become more pronounced and with this sign rising it will be a good time to work perseveringly, as this will bring its own reward and there will surely be success and a promotion to a more permanently satisfactory position. It also tends to make relations with one's employers, or those with whom one has to deal in the business world, more mutually satisfactory and binding, bringing something of affection, or at least of respect and regard, which will make such dealings happier and more successful in every way.

Third Decanate; rulers, Saturn and Mercury.—This, too, is a good combination and one which will awaken greater thought in all business affairs. There should be more discretion and discrimination shown, though in the ordinary horoscope it will tend to increase the selfishness of the native, as Saturn, in the general sense, is selfishness personified, and when there is strong contact with the mental planet, it causes more *thought* on self and self-interests. It gives tact and diplomacy and the ability to carry plans to a far-distant goal, but in doing so the native may become overanxious and worried and, other influences in the chart agreeing, ill health will ensue, in all probability taking the form of indigestion, stomach or bowel trouble.

Aquarius.

First Decanate; ruler, Uranus.—This new sign should bring an entire change both of thought and conditions into the life. The general trend of events will change, and the changes will come with greater suddenness and unexpectedness. From living the rather selfish, self-centered life that Capricorn is apt to cause, the thoughts and aspirations will go out towards others. There will be the inclination to join societies, to make new friends, or to connect up again with the old ones that have been dropped while the business of money-making held the attention, and the whole intellectual and mental standpoint will be raised a notch, causing a more humane attitude towards other people as a consequence. With this will come a better understanding of human nature and a desire to work along some distinctly philanthropic lines. Of course, in an afflicted chart, this will not be so evident, and in that case the native will need to be careful in these matters, lest he get into trouble through those pretending to be his friends, and who make a show of helping him. In such charts this new sign can bring a good deal of misfortune and trouble, undesirable emotional experiences and unfortunate friendships.

Second Decanate; rulers, Uranus and Mercury.—All the tendencies of the first decanate will now be more manifest on the mental plane. The philanthropic desires will be planned with more thought and intelligence. It is likely that something of this sort will be undertaken, which will necessitate traveling or correspondence. All things will be attended to with more thoughtfulness and detail. This is a very good influence for those who are really idealistic and anxious for the welfare of others, for they will be better able to discriminate and judge of the best thing to be done for those who need their help. New friends will be made among those who are studious or literary and there should be much pleasure and advantage in such associations.

Third Decanate; rulers, Uranus and Venus.—This, of course, will bring greater love and affection. Therefore, it is easy to see how further advanced one may become who is already along the right path. The desire to do for others, awakened by the influence of this sign, grows intellectually and thoughtfully through the second decanate, and now comes real, sincere love for both the work itself and for those for whom the work is done. It brings the love onto a mental plane where there will be a greater sense of justice and cooperation and thus both the native and those whom he desires to help will benefit on all planes. He will become more closely linked with others, will know what true friendship is in a way that he has never known before, and there will be a better balance of judgment and feeling than there has ever been.

Pisces.

First Decanate; ruler, Neptune.—Arriving at the possible point brought about through the Uranian-Venus influence, the individual should now be at the place where he is willing to sacrifice all that he has. This spiritual sign of Pisces is the point of one's own undoing. It brings the inevitable, the difficult experiences, the karmic conditions, and the awakening of the soul to higher things and to greater possibilities. While this sign is on the ascendant, conditions will not be easy. Sorrows and disappointments will be encountered and others will require comfort and help at the sacrifice of one's own needs and comfort. There will be connections with hospitals and institutions and the generally hampering and restricting influence which this sign brings will, if the nativity agrees, cause the native to be confined in some such place himself.

Second Decanate; rulers, Neptune and the Moon.—Now is a time when one is liable to become extremely sensitive and even morbid, if there is a natural inclination that way. The sympathies will be aroused and it will be hard to keep thoughts of the sufferings of others from affecting one's own health and spirits. There will be many domestic experiences, perhaps of an unhappy nature, though if there are no special afflictions, it will bring romance and some very pleasing attachments. The tendency will be towards greater emotion and sensitiveness in every way, and cause one to be more psychic and mediumistic. It is also possible to become too receptive and easily influenced by others and it will, in that case, be necessary to fortify oneself by a more positive attitude of mind to prevent the thoughts and conditions of others from getting too great a hold on the emotions, which would surely end by creating an abnormally nervous, even neurotic, condition.

Third Decanate; rulers, Neptune and Mars.—The combination of Neptune and Mars is by no means a harmonious one. A good deal will depend upon the natural tendencies of the native, for this decanate will bring a fight between the desires and passions of the flesh and the aspirations and longings of the soul. The effect will be to cause a good deal of confusion and anxiety and a generally trying time. At such a time a good deal of "Karma" may be precipitated and it requires a well-balanced character to get through this period without the emotional strain being too great for the health and nervous system. At such a period, the low will fall lower, and those who are progressing will have a hard time to keep their equilibrium and maintain the standard they have set for themselves. It is only the very advanced who will come through with little effect, unless, at the time that this sign and decan are in the ascendant, the other influences of the Progressed Chart are such as to give considerable aid.

CHAPTER 7.

THE PROGRESSED MOON.

The position of the Moon for the Progressed Chart is found in the same manner as are the planets for the Natal Chart. When this is done the number of the degrees and minutes of the daily motion is divided by twelve for the twelve months of the year, and this will give the position of the Moon for each month.

Here is an example showing the calculations for Chart No. 2; progressed birth date, for 1928, is April 5, 1870:

Moon's position April 6, 1870..		15° 43′ Gemini
Moon's position April 5, 1870..	3° 40′	3° 40′ Gemini
Moon's daily motion..........		12° 03′
Logarithm for daily motion...	.2992	
Constant logarithm	.4491	
Correction logarithm	.7483=4° 17′	
Moon's position on progressed birthday		7° 57′ Gemini

The motion of the Moon from that day (or year) to the next is twelve degrees and three minutes, which, divided by twelve for the twelve months of the year, gives a motion for each month of one degree and fifteen seconds. Add this increment to the position of the Moon for the birthday, February 6, 1928, and you will have the positions for each succeeding month. Thus:

February 6, 1928..	7° 57′ 00″	April 6, 1928	9° 57′ 30″
	1° 00′ 15″		1° 00′ 15″
March 6, 1928....	8° 57′ 15″	May 6, 1928......	10° 57′ 45″
	1° 00′ 15″		1° 00′ 15″
April 6, 1928.....	9° 57′ 30″	June 6, 1928......	11° 58′ 00″

(68)

June 6, 1928......11° 58' 00"
                   1° 00' 15"

July 6, 1928......12° 58' 15"
                   1° 00' 15"

August 6, 1928...13° 58' 30"
                   1° 00' 15"

September 6, 1928.14° 58' 45"
                    1° 00' 15"

October 6, 1928...15° 59' 00"

October 6, 1928...15° 59' 00"
                   1° 00' 15"

November 6, 1928.16° 59' 15"
                   1° 00' 15"

December 6, 1928.17° 59' 30"
                   1° 00' 15"

January 6, 1929...18° 59' 45"

House Position.

Too much reliance should not be placed upon the action of the progressed Moon, for, while sometimes she will make her presence felt very strongly, at other times her influence is scarcely noticeable, even though the Moon may be making quite a powerful aspect. As a general rule, however, she will act true to form, in some manner or other, for it is only those who are more advanced than the majority, and more individual than personal, who are able to overcome the influences of the lunar orb. As is well known, the Moon rules the personality, and it is those people who are absorbed in themselves, who deal in the smaller and personal things of life and who are small and changeable in their thoughts and ideas, who feel more directly the effects of the Moon, either in the nativity, the Progressed Chart or the transits. Therefore, the further we get away from this, the larger we grow and the less we feel the tantalizing and changeable influence of the Moon. It is not that all her aspects are adverse. Far from it. But, to a great extent, we can do without them, for they do not specially tend towards a spiritual or permanent growth and for the most part are concerned with the mundane affairs of life, and therefore are temporal and ephemeral.

When the Moon is found in the third house of the Natal Chart, the effects of the progressed Moon will be felt most on the lower mental plane, though, to some extent, it will affect all the material affairs. When it is in the second house it will have to do with the finances, and so on through all the houses, but it will be tempered and modified by the house position of the progressed Moon herself, causing the whole personal life, however, to be accentuated when she returns to the house of her radical position.   Before considering the aspects of the progressed Moon, we will take her house positions, which will, of course, always be stronger when she is in her own house, the fourth; her own signs, Cancer or Taurus; or in the house in which we find her in the nativity.

Moon in First House.

The Moon progressing through the first house, especially when crossing the cusp, is sure to bring a definite change of some kind, either a journey or a change of residence, habits or some of the conditions which closely concern the personal life.   When the Moon or the ascendant is afflicted in the nativity, especially in a woman's chart, the health is likely to be considerably affected and a change will have to be made in the life because of this, leading to many other changes. Under such conditions, if the Moon should pass over Mars, or make a bad aspect to Mars, an operation or a fever will be the result.   Care should be taken as to the changes made, for unless the aspects of the Moon are very good, her influence is not conducive to the best judgment.   The native is now likely to pay more attention to material affairs and to those that belong to the lower plane and the lower mind, unless he is determined to raise himself up by the channels open in other parts of the horoscope.

Moon in Second House.

The Moon in the second house has to do with finances more than any other thing.   This brings a period when money will engross one more than usual and also brings opportunities for making more money. The method of making the money will depend upon the nature of the aspects the Moon may make and the promise of the nativity, as well as the general directions for the year.   If the aspect should be a good one to Jupiter in the fifth house, there would be excellent chances for success in speculations; if to Saturn in the fourth, it would be a favorable aspect for buying a home or to deal in real estate or engage in mining. But if the aspects were adverse, that would be the time to avoid doing those same things, though gain could come the very same month if the Moon was making a good aspect to a planet in another part of the horoscope.

Moon in Third House.

The Moon in the third house will bring into activity those things indicated by this house, so that one would expect the mind to be more active and also more restless, since the Moon is of such a fickle nature. If there is any natural tendency towards depression, this position of the Moon will add to it and there will be dissatisfaction, restlessness, irritability and contention, if such are promised in the nativity. The mind will be busy all the time, and so some new studies, new interests, industries or hobbies should be undertaken as a safety valve for this energy. Relatives are likely to play a more important part in the life, and the outcome of any closer contact with them will depend upon the aspects that the Moon makes during its stay here. A conjunction with Saturn, for instance, could bring the death of an older brother, or it could bring a depressed state of mind or a steadying influence in regard to one's duties and occupation, according to the other indications at the time.

Moon in Fourth House.

The Moon in the fourth house has to do with the home environment and brings fresh activities in this direction. It rarely occurs without bringing a change of some kind in this connection. It may be either a change of residence or a change of conditions which might alter the arrangements in the home and make them more unsettled. Care should be taken at the times that the aspects are unfavorable, for there will be danger of making some very unwise move and doing the things that will spoil future prospects for peace and happiness in the home. Since this house also rules property, real estate and mining, the same precautions will be necessary in regard to these matters, but if everything is promising in the nativity and there are good lunar aspects, it will be a good time to invest, sell or trade in these things. The fourth house represents the midnight point and is therefore one of the psychic and occult houses, so that, with the Moon in this position, especially if contacting one of the occult planets, there should be some psychic experiences, a revelation of some kind, or at least an awakening in this direction. At such a time much may be learned if the native is steady enough and has a definite purpose towards further development along these lines.

Moon in Fifth House.

The Moon in the fifth house, which is the house of children, love affairs, amusements and speculation, will affect the individual in whatever manner is open along these various lines. It frequently brings about love affairs, or at any rate awakens the emotions in some way, and brings opportunities for expressing the feelings and affections in directions probably not known before. To a woman it may bring the birth of a child and, according to the promises in the nativity, may bring sorrow, joy or new experiences with regard to children. It is a time when care should be taken in regard to all investments and speculations, for the Moon being of such a restless and unsettled nature, the outcome of such activities will be very doubtful unless the aspects are particularly favorable. This being the house that rules the feelings and emotions, all the activities of the native should be checked up by reason, for in allowing too much play of the emotions they are more likely to incline him to do the unwise thing and thus spoil many of his future opportunities.

Moon in Sixth House.

The Moon in the sixth house has a very important bearing upon the health. To those who are naturally sensitive, any unfavorable aspects of the Moon while passing through this house, especially if they be to Mercury or Neptune, will cause an increase in sensitiveness and the result will show itself in indigestion, psychic disorders or a nervous breakdown. Even to the more hardy ones there is a tendency to sickness of some kind, and it is well for all people, while the Moon is in this house, unless very well aspected, to be rather more careful of the diet than usual and to avoid such environments as are at all injurious. Particularly should care be given to the selection of the places where they eat and sleep. Other people will have more effect upon them on the psychic plane, and thus the drain upon their nervous energy may be very much greater than they have any idea of and may finally show itself in some disorder of the body, depending upon the natural weakness of the sixth house or of the ascendant. This house also rules the employment and those who are inferior, and the same care should be given in regard to these matters when the aspects of the Moon are bad, but when they are good, it will be a time to become better established in employment or to seek advantages elsewhere. It will also be the time to employ servants or other workers. Fresh air, exercise and hygiene should be given more consideration than ever while the Moon is in this house, particularly if the Moon is afflicted in the nativity.

Moon in Seventh House.

The Moon in the seventh house will bring new connections with other people, partnerships, opportunities to connect up with some corporation, or to become more closely associated with lawyers, depending upon the status, age and outlet of the native. To those who are of marriageable age, the Moon coming to the cusp of this house, or making a strong aspect therein, is likely to bring about marriage, and even to those already married it will frequently bring some other person into the life to whom they will become greatly attached and with whom they will desire to become more closely associated. To those who are in business and desire to form partnerships, such times as the Moon is making good aspects from this house will be very favorable for them, but consideration should be given to the promise of the nativity as to whether partnerships of any kind could ever be permanently satisfactory or profitable.

Moon in Eighth House.

The Moon in the eighth house, which is the house of death, tends to bring a death in the family or to make active some affairs connected with death. The Moon making a bad aspect while in this position usually brings death. The judgment should be guided as to whose death it will be, according to the house which is aspected. For instance, if it is the third house, it is likely to be a brother or sister to whom death will occur; if the eleventh, it will be a friend; if the tenth, the mother or employer; and so on through any of the houses. The good aspects bring gains through death, legacies, gifts, insurance or something of that kind, and since this, like the fourth house, is also one of the occult houses, it will bring some new experiences, a keener psychic sense, an increased interest in all occult subjects, and those who are quite advanced along these lines should experience a development of the inner senses and some activity on the psychic plane. If the aspects do not work out in any of these ways, they will be directed towards the money affairs of the partner, either for good or ill, according to the nature of the aspects and the promise of the Natal Chart.

Moon in Ninth House.

The Moon in the ninth house is perhaps one of its best positions, because this is the house of aspiration and idealism, and the Moon, ruling the personality, has the opportunities to grow and expand towards the individuality and thus raise the whole of the lower nature to a higher plane. To those who are striving towards the higher life, this position gives greater opportunities, and every effort should be made to make all the progress possible, while there is so little resistance, towards the goal. This is also the house of long journeys, and so there are better opportunities for travel while the Moon is in this house than at any other time. There are, of course, many times when the horoscope or the prevailing conditions prevent travel, and therefore the vibrations work along the lines of aspiration, and also long flights of imagination and fancy may take the place of journeys on the physical plane. For those of an orthodox and conservative turn of mind there will be an increased interest in religion, and for those who are scientific, the thoughts will be more definitely directed along these lines, while those who are immersed in such things may make some great discoveries.

Moon in Tenth House.

The Moon in the tenth house is also a good position; especially if the nativity is a good one and the directions for the year favorable, for it tends to bring advantageous changes in business, to advance the public status of the native and to give him opportunities for progress in the directions along which his efforts are directed. Business affairs will assume greater importance, and if there are good aspects, it will be an excellent time to make any important changes in business, profession or with employers. A good aspect of the Moon to the Sun or Jupiter at this time will be an excellent opportunity to seek promotion, an increase in salary or an advancement of some kind. The tenth house, having also to do with the mother, will probably tend to bring her affairs more prominently into the life, and an adverse aspect of the Moon might mean trouble with, or through, her in some manner; or even sickness or death to her, depending upon the nature of the aspected planet and its position.

Moon in Eleventh House.

The Moon in the eleventh house turns the activities towards friends. It is a good time to deal more definitely with them, either in a business way or in any other manner that is desired—provided, of course, that the rest of the horoscope agrees. If the Moon is passing through the eleventh house, and during that time makes a good aspect to Jupiter or Venus in the second, one could be reasonably sure of gains, both financial or otherwise, through friends. If making aspects to the first house, there will be personal advantages through friends, and so on through all the houses. Hopes and wishes also come under the rule of the eleventh house, and according to the present aspects and the natal promise of the Moon, they will now either be fulfilled or dashed to the ground.

Moon in Twelfth House.

The Moon in the twelfth house is not so good, even though it be quite well aspected, for it tends to bring one into touch with a certain amount of sorrow and suffering, even though it may not be directed to oneself. If there is an afflicted nativity, it will go quite hard with the native unless the aspects at the time are unusually good, because this position tends to bring "fate", or "karma"—conditions or events over which we have, at the time, no control. It gives opportunities for strengthening and deepening the inner nature, and the experiences are usually such as may turn one to a more earnest inquiry into the meaning of life. It is the house that has to do with hospitals, asylums and all places of confinement, and thus it may be that the native either has to enter one of these places himself, or else has much to do with those who are there to whom he might be of service. Aspects and their nature as well as the nature of the planets involved will be the deciding factors in such cases. If there were an opposition to Mars in the sixth house, an operation would be most likely to take place—of course, in a hospital. If there were a square to Saturn in the fourth house, it could mean an imprisonment, either to the native or to his father. But these events would only occur if the nativity gave such promise. Otherwise it might mean an extra burden thrown upon the native, causing him anxiety and possibly sickness, so that he would find it necessary to retire for a time in order to recover.

The student must always know the Radical Chart first, with its possibilities and tendencies, before he can be ·capable of predicting, with any degree of accuracy, the direction through which any particular person will work through the aspects of his Progressed Chart. While, as we have said, the progressed Moon is not always of such great importance, it may be so if it awakens, in an evil chart, the promises of the nativity. But, even though a nativity be afflicted, if the man himself is advancing along higher lines, these positions will not affect him to so great an extent.

CHAPTER 8.

ASPECTS BY THE PROGRESSION OF THE MOON.

From here on, throughout this treatise, what is said in relation to the effect of aspects is to be applied to all aspects made by progressions and transits, whether by progressed with radical, progressed to progressed, transiting to radical or transiting to progressed.

In most cases the effects will be stronger when the aspects are directed to the planets in the nativity, though not always so, for much depends on the type of person and his natural response to old or new conditions.

Aspects by progression or transit have only a very limited orb; rarely more than one degree, and with the transits of the faster-moving planets the aspects are usually only effective when exact.

Sometimes, however, the progressed Sun or Moon will have an influence while still two degrees distant, but this only when some transit comes to hasten or delay the action of those planets in what has already been promised by progression.

One other exception may be stated here and that is in regard to the transits of the slow-moving planets, Neptune, Uranus and Saturn. These planets are so powerful under certain conditions that they will act more or less continuously for years. Take, for instance, the example shown in Plate 1. The transit of Saturn toward the end of 1920, when he crossed the radical Ascendant and remained close there for almost twelve months. During all that time the native's health was considerably affected and it was not until Jupiter came to his aid in the fall of 1921 by also transiting over the Ascendant that his health came back to normal. Business conditions with him were also in a very depressed state during that time.

The Moon acts as the medium whereby the Solar and mutual aspects, either in the Radical or the Progressed Charts, may find expression. The Moon may make some very strong aspects, either for good or ill, and yet the months may pass without any appreciable effects, the cause being found in the fact that there is no need for expression from those directions since the rest of the chart is not inclined that way. But when we find the planetary influences are such that they coincide with the lunar influences for any given month, there will then be noticeable results, and the month will be a more or less critical one, according to the strength and nature of the vibrations. The conjunction of the Moon to the planets is, in a general way, the most powerful of all the aspects and the one that is most likely to precipitate events and bring them about with promptness and precision. Of the good aspects the trine is the strongest, the sextile being next, followed by the quincunx, and finally the semi-sextile and quintile—though these latter two are of very little importance and need only be considered when they add weight to some similar testimony. Of the evil aspects the square is the strongest, the opposition next, and finally the semi-square and the sesquiquadrate. The conjunction and opposition are not wholly good or evil, for the effects depend upon the nature of the planet aspected and the promise of the nativity. Thus, if the Moon comes to an opposition of Venus in the Progressed Chart and there is a trine of these two in the radix, then, unless the native is of a low, unprogressive type, the effects can be almost wholly beneficial, for it is then acting as an open door for the benefits of the radix to flow through. The same can be said of the conjunction. The Moon coming to the conjunction of an evilly aspected planet in the nativity, even though it be a benefic planet, may have distinctly adverse effects, while the conjunction to a malefic may be quite beneficial if such is the promise in the Natal Chart. Again, in regard to the aspects of the Moon, much will depend upon the strength of the planet and as to whether it indicates a strong or a weak personality. Some aspects will affect a female more than a male, especially in regard to the health. The Moon, being a changeable, fickle planet, is very readily affected by close proximity to another planet, but the effects are not so deep or so lasting.

The Moon in Conjunction or Parallel with the Sun.

This is an influence that is usually felt very distinctly in the Progressed Chart. With a female it will affect the health and cause lassitude, lack of vitality, or make more pronounced any natural ailment. Apart from that the influence is good and will bring some decided change into the life, either in thought, habit or environment. The general tendency is towards a transfer, and therefore usually means a change of residence, though it may be a change on any plane and in any or all directions, and should be read, as far as possible, in the terms of the prevailing influences. The feeling is always towards change, but it is not always that the opportunities correspond, and so the result may be merely restlessness, plannings and arrangements. If other things agree, it is a very good time for all personal matters, and undertakings may be accomplished at this time to great advantage. In short, it is a favorable time for new plans, new undertakings, friendships and partnerships. Even marriage may be consummated with benefit to all concerned.

Moon in Good Aspect to the Sun.

This usually brings a period of happiness and success. The health of either male or female will be improved, and all matters that have to do with home or business will be really benefited. It is an appropriate time for expansion in any direction, and all opportunities for development should be pushed as far as possible. It brings a more peaceful state of mind, clearer vision, better judgment and firmer resolutions. All relations with employers, superiors and those who have any authority will be more satisfactory, and it is a suitable time to seek advancement, raise in pay, fresh fields and favors. There are few better influences than the good aspects of the Sun and Moon, for they help in every phase of life and affect the spiritual, as well as the material, life of the individual.

The Moon in Bad Aspect to the Sun.

This tends to bring about estrangements and separations, upsetting the domestic life and frequently bringing trouble with, or through, one of the parents. It is very unfavorable for dealings with superiors, employers, and even for social affairs. Depending upon the strength of the aspect, there may be trouble endangering one's honor or reputation and, since the contact is separative in its nature, it may bring a parting from a loved one through death, misunderstanding, or some unfortunate circumstance. The parting, of course, could come through the native himself being removed, since the influence distinctly tends towards change. Also it brings many anxieties, annoyances, ill health and even sickness serious enough to make hospital treatment necessary.

The Moon in Conjunction, Parallel or Good Aspect with Mercury.

Remembering that Mercury is the mental planet, it is easily understood that the Moon with this planet will quicken the processes of the mind and that there will be a stronger link between the mind and the brain. It will give the native opportunities to develop his latent talents, and any abilities that he might have for writing, selling, buying or trading will become more manifest. He will be more thoughtful and at the same time more mentally active, while his wits will be quicker and his memory better. The conjunction is not so good for concentration, because there is a tendency for the mind to be too active and dissipative; but this will be more than made up for by the keenness, enterprise and quickness of the mind. This is the time for writing, correspondence, lectures, study courses and all things that require an active and inquiring mind. It is also good for travel, and journeys begun when the Moon is in good aspect to Mercury, other influences being agreeable, are sure to turn out well and profitably. Much, of course, will depend upon the ability of the native to use these good vibrations beneficially, as to whether the effects will be permanent or transitory.

The Moon in Adverse Aspect to Mercury.

Under this aspect care should be observed. It will be an unsatisfactory time to start any new undertakings, to correspond, sign papers or contracts, start journeys or new projects. Particularly is it bad for negotiations with other people in the way of selling or trading, and if possible, it is best to leave all such matters till the vibrations have passed. With those who are naturally nervous and highly strung it goes much harder, and it is well for such people to keep quiet and not exert themselves more than is necessary.

The Moon in Conjunction, Parallel or Good Aspect with Venus.

This is a particularly good influence, especially for all matters that have to do with the social side of life, with friendships and with those who are of the Venus type. It is a good time to form any kind of union, especially marriages, and, in fact, often brings marriage about, especially in a man's horoscope. Everything goes well at such a time. All things seem more cheerful and buoyant—and benefits, pleasures and gifts all come more freely, especially to those who have Venus as their ruler, or well posited in the nativity. The native should feel happier, more contented and at peace, and will be able to better and more freely express his emotions and feelings. It will tend to draw to him those who understand him, who have sympathy for him and who vibrate in harmony with himself. It usually has a bearing upon the finances also, and is a good time to spend money, make investments recommended by friends, and to go shopping for clothes, finery, jewelry and all things that go towards adornment, either of person or home. It increases business for those who have such an outlet, and life is gayer and happier in every way. This is noticeable in the world generally at such times as there are good aspects ephemerally. We find that there are then more social events, invitations, more flowers bought and sold, on those days than on any others.

The Moon in Adverse Aspect to Venus.

This tends to cause trouble in matters where one's feelings and emotions are involved. It is unsatisfactory for dealing with those to whom one is bound by affection, for it brings an oversensitive condition, little misunderstandings and happenings that wound one more easily than at other times. It is unfavorable for dealings with the opposite sex; is a poor time to propose marriage, or to consider any actions that are not wholly moral or conventional. It can cause trouble in the home, with friends or parents, brings disappointments and disagreements with others and generally creates an inharmonious period.

The Moon in Good Aspect to Mars.

Any aspect of the Moon to Mars tends to cause rashness of action, impulse and passion. But to those who know how to handle the strong forces of Mars, this vibration is exceedingly good and can help them in many ways. It will make the native more enterprising and ambitious, giving him more force and daring, and thus enable him to do things and get to places that at another time he would not even consider. It is a good time for starting new plans, for travel, for making quick changes and for all things that require courage, adventure and vitality. It is a strong force and needs wisdom to direct it to the best use.

The Moon in Conjunction, Parallel or Adverse Aspect to Mars.

The energy that comes from these aspects is hard to control, and the greatest caution is required to prevent the native from doing the rash and impulsive thing that later he will surely regret. It is no time to form hasty decisions, and the resolve should be to sleep on all matters of any importance. There will be an increase of both physical and mental energy and these should be carefully directed, for otherwise they might lead to quarrels, extremes of action, passion, anger and perversion of all the Mars qualities. Also, these aspects frequently bring sickness, accidents or operations. It is not a wise or safe time to travel, and important dealings with others should be delayed until the vibrations are more harmonious.

The Moon in Conjunction, Parallel or Good Aspect to Jupiter.

Jupiter being the greatest benefic, the good angles of the Moon to this planet should give the greatest blessings and opportunities. Therefore, one may look for a prosperous period when all things will go well, when one will feel more hopeful and buoyant, and when success is the outcome of every effort. Such a time as this is the most promising for starting new undertakings, making alterations and arrangements, getting before the public and for pressing along lines that have hitherto been closed. It always has a definite influence on the financial side, and unless Jupiter is weakly placed or heavily afflicted in the nativity, it brings more prosperity and greater success than promised by any other lunar influence. To those who are naturally religiously inclined or markedly orthodox and ceremonial, the tendencies in these directions will be increased and there will be an added pompousness and egotism. But even behind this there is kindliness, honor and uprightness. To those who are truly spiritual, it increases the perception and throws new light on many of the inner thoughts. However, it must be remembered that the benefits will rarely act on all the planes. Thus, those who desire material things above everything else will get them, and for those to whom spiritual growth is the more desirable, the perception and understanding will be bountifully increased. The choice is the individual's, but it is seldom that he can have both. The choice, naturally, is not necessarily a conscious one, but works automatically, according to the general nature of the desires.

The Moon in Adverse Aspect to Jupiter.

This, of course, works in the opposite direction and always brings a loss of some kind. For the most part it is financial, and for that reason it is a most unfavorable time for speculations, for making investments or for indulging in any kind of extravagance. So often it is the inclination of the native to be extravagant at such a time, to throw care and discretion to the winds and to go to extremes in a manner he would not consider wise when in his normal condition. Instead, this is a time when everything should be taken quietly, when it will be ill-advised to make any changes, to travel, start anything new or push affairs in any direction. Domestic and social affairs will be less harmonious, and those who have any tendency to liver trouble should avoid eating those things which could cause an excess of bile, or that could clog the liver. Less food should be taken and it should be of a cooling and simple nature. It is an unfavorable time to lend or borrow money or to allow feelings of generosity to overrule the judgment.

The Moon in Good Aspect to Saturn.

Saturn being the planet of steadiness and responsibility, brings these attributes to the personality when the Moon makes good aspects to him. He brings a keener sense of duty, a response to the claims of those who are older and who have any right to demand or command. Conditions tend to become calmer and more harmonious under such an influence and yet, at the same time, there may be a steady pull upwards, for it is often that promotion, honor, respect or advancement may be offered one who is surrounded by such vibrations. Whatever of progress there may be will be sure, and the advantages will be more permanent than if they came at any other time. Nothing will be rapid and it might often seem as though delay were the main feature. But while slow, it will be sure, and the benefits will not vanish into thin air as soon as the influence passes. Whatever effort can be made to establish a steadier and more secure future should be done at such a time as this, and recognition and friendships with those who are older will be well worth while.

The Moon in Conjunction, Parallel or Evil Aspect to Saturn.

This is a depressing influence. Usually some sorrowful experience comes at such a time. Sometimes it is a death, sometimes a misunderstanding or a keen disappointment, but more often it brings obstacles, and delays the native in obtaining satisfactory results from his efforts. Delay is the main feature, even to delaying the unsatisfactory results of this influence! We have known such an event as a death to delay three months from the time of the square of the Moon to Saturn because of the natural tendency of this planet to hold matters up. Depression is another strong feature of this contact—depression of mind, spirits, body and finances. There will be depression in whatever line is open to Saturn's attack, and of course the result is that it rarely fails to bring despondency of mind. This shows most in those who are easily depressed, and it is a continuance of such influences—as the Sun square to Saturn in the general directions and the Moon making a similar aspect during the year—that causes long illness or chronic complaints, the outcome of which is despondency and occasionally suicide. We do not mean that this will always be the result, but it is these vibrations of Saturn that do cause such sad events in those who are not mentally elastic or buoyant enough to be able to resist his hard and unremitting onslaughts.

The Moon in Good Aspect to Uranus.

An entirely different result is derived from the combination of these two, compared to that of the Moon and Saturn. Instead of delay, steadiness and calmness, we get rush, excitement, surprise and change. The magnetic currents of the personality are increased and there is a greater attraction towards other people. Thus unexpected contacts result; new friendships are made, or a chance meeting which will alter the whole tenor of one's life occurs. Such are the results of the Uranian vibrations. Where Saturn will cause one to withdraw and be rather more isolated than usual, Uranus will throw one among people, cause one to join groups, societies, or brotherhoods, and instead of settling still more securely into a groove, he will break up the existing conditions and bring new plans, ideas and promises into one's life, completely changing the old order of things. Sudden gains, changes, journeys and all such events may happen under this influence and the results are usually very advantageous, even for those who do not usually care for change. The nervous system is stimulated, and to those who are interested in any of the higher systems of thought there comes new impulse, newer and more original ideas and a mental and spiritual stimulus that helps to raise such persons to a higher plane of consciousness.

The Moon Conjunct, Parallel or in Adverse Aspect to Uranus.

The conjunction and parallel are not necessarily evil to those who are able to operate on the higher planes of thought; but for the ordinary person there is an element of danger in the conjunction, because the close contact stirs the personality to do the unexpected and indiscreet thing and to act with an impulse that often causes regrets later. All the aspects of the Moon with Uranus are fraught with the danger of impulsive and indiscreet action because of the very nature of the planet, which is wayward and unconventional. For this reason, its evil aspects are naturally quite dangerous. Thus, it is necessary to be much more guarded in all association with those of the opposite sex. The magnetic forces will be stronger than usual, as is also the case with the good aspects, but the tendency will be to attract the wrong type of persons and to make associations that will be detrimental, either to the morals or accepted conventions of the day. At such times it is most unwise to consider making any changes, though often changes will come because of these influences without the action of the native himself. One should be on guard and prepared for the "unexpected," so as to avoid doing the thing that is unwise through being taken by surprise. It is a time when domestic conditions could be disarranged, when disagreements or separations may take place and when unexpected difficulties of one kind and another may present themselves. The native himself will be more nervous, irritable, and impatient, with less self-control than usual and lacking in the calmness and forethought that could keep him straight. He will have queer fancies and new and fantastic ideas which usually are quite impossible, and he will strain at the leash in order to break whatever bonds are holding him. Not because he dislikes the bonds, but because he wants to feel himself free.

The Moon in Conjunction, Parallel or Good Aspect to Neptune.

The conjunction in this case also is not always entirely good, but for the most part it is—because if the native is not able to respond to this vibration in the right way, he often feels it not at all. It rarely passes, however, without making the native more sensitive and impressionable to the conditions and people that surround him. To those who are sensitive to the vibrations from other planes there may be some awakening, some vivid dream or vision or some other unusual psychic experience. The influence renders most people much more receptive, and it is therefore favorable for mediumistic experiments, psychometry, the study of dreams and psychism and for the study of unusual people or conditions, since one is often drawn towards those who are different or peculiar.

The Moon in Adverse Aspect to Neptune.

This can bring some very trying conditions and events into the life, according to the natural tendencies of the horoscope and the houses in which the aspect falls. It always makes the native supersensitive and very impressionable. He feels vibrations more keenly and is more easily upset by close contact with other people. For that reason care should be taken in choosing associations and places to eat and sleep, while under such influences. Frequently it will bring one into touch with undesirables; either fraudulent people, deformed people, or those who will sap one's energy or vitality. Uncanny psychic experiences often come, as well as queer happenings, estrangements or sorrowful events—all those things that are out of the usual and which do not happen in the regular course of events.

The Moon Progressed to an Aspect of Her Natal Place.

This brings some sort of a change which is of minor importance unless stimulated by other influences of a like nature. The character of the changes will depend on the position of the Moon at birth and the house from which the progressed Moon makes the aspect. As, for instance, from the first house there will be changes in habits, in personal affairs, in physical conditions and perhaps in environment though not necessarily in residence. From the second house changes in regard to money. From the fourth house changes in connection with the home and so on through the various houses.

Good aspects will bring benefits through changes or through personal matters. Adverse aspects will bring undesirable changes or undesirable personal conditions. The progression of the Moon to conjunction of her natal place is good, providing the Moon at birth is not heavily afflicted.

CHAPTER 9.

ASPECTS BY THE PROGRESSION OF THE SUN.

The Sun is, of course, the dominant influence in any Progressed Horoscope and if the aspects are good, the other influences have very much less weight. As a result the year will prove to be a beneficial one, taken as a whole. The Sun is the vitality of the chart and from him all things have their life and being and it is at his suggestion, so to speak, that all influences begin to work upon the native. Therefore, if he is in agreement, then it is well; if he decrees otherwise, it takes a tremendous lot of beneficence from the rest of the planets to oppose his will. It is the Sun that brings the epochs in an individual's life, and his aspects mark the periods or milestones in the path of evolution. It is at his instigation that we proceed along new lines and enter into new cycles of experience, and that is why his aspects are so important and hold dominance over all the others.

The Sun in Good Aspect to Mars.

This increases the independent spirit of the native and brings the impulse to start off in some new and more enterprising manner, using newer and more daring methods and attempting things that he would not consider possible at any other time. This is really a very fine vibration, for it brings renewed vitality, better health (because the blood flows more freely), and a great deal of energy and bodily activity. It is a time when events will happen with greater rapidity and with more force. It is as if there were a strong stimulus from without working upon one's affairs, and one's own temperament will be more ardent and the actions performed in a more forceful, strenuous and passionate manner. For those who have Mars strong in the nativity, some care is needed so as not to become too bold, dominant and passionate. For those who have their own lower nature well under control, this is a splendid influence for progress and health.

(88)

The Sun in Adverse Aspect to Mars.

This brings a very critical time, especially when the aspect is the conjunction, square or opposition. The greatest care is necessary to preserve an equilibrium and to prevent things from going wrong. Caution should now be the watchword, for the same force and ambition will be working as in the case of the good aspects, but it will be much harder to direct them into the proper channels. There is some danger of accidents, imprudent actions that could lead to serious trouble, ill health or quarrels. No changes of a vital nature should be made while the Sun has such an aspect to Mars, especially changes of the nature of the house in which Mars or the Sun is situated. For instance, in the tenth house, no change should be made in business or occupation; in the fourth, no changes in the home, and so on. Quarrels, disputes and arguments are all likely to occur under this influence, and may be serious enough to result in domestic trouble, estrangements and dishonor.

The Sun in Good Aspect to Venus.

This is one of the best influences for marriage, especially when it occurs in conjunction in a woman's chart. It brings a cheerful atmosphere and one is always more hopeful and gay under such rays. It also brings a time when things go right with much less trouble. There are not the same hindrances or opposition, and it is much easier for the native to be cheerful and optimistic. The vibrations operating within the native cause him to send out loving and happy thoughts, and these naturally find a response in the hearts of those about him, so that there is more love, sympathy and affection shown than is usual in that particular life. It is usually considered by astrologers that a good aspect of the Sun to Venus brings the happiest and most peaceful period in the native's life, and that the conjunction is perhaps the most powerful aspect. In any case, it helps to bring prosperity, and most things started and worked upon during such an influence will have a happy and beneficial ending.

The Sun in Adverse Aspect to Venus.

This naturally tends to have the opposite effect to the good vibrations of the Sun to Venus. Instead of everything going very happily, things seem to go wrong and are disappointing. Venus being the planet of love and affection, it is in this direction that the influence will be most felt and thus the native will take things to heart, will fret over conditions because they are not what he expected them to be, and will find less sympathy and affection among his friends, which will cause him sorrow. It must be remembered, however, that unless Venus is much afflicted in the nativity, evil aspects to such a benefic planet cannot have a very serious effect—not like an evil aspect of the Sun to Saturn, for instance. But it will, under certain conditions, cause separations from loved ones, and, in a woman's chart, will often cause the death of husband or child, or bring some other saddening influence into the home. Presumably, all evil aspects of any of the planets tend to have a separating and disintegrating effect, and so, even with these two planets, there can be separation from friends, employer, money, lover, personal possessions, or ill health, depending upon the house and sign position of either planet, and on the promise of the nativity. To those who are sensitive and who depend upon affection and demonstration of love, this can become, instead of the happiest period of the life, as promised by the good aspects, the saddest and most forlorn. It is never a good time for domestic affairs, nor for launching out into any financial enterprises, and for those who marry at such a time there is little promise of permanent happiness.

The Sun in Good Aspect to Mercury.

This brings all the mental activities into play and makes the period of the Sun's progressive aspects to this planet an excellent time to start new studies, to enter a university, begin important writings, especially if they are likely to take a considerable time, and to push all affairs that have to do with correspondence or communications of any kind. Important changes may be made during this time, journeys taken, new duties undertaken, and to those who are working on the higher mental planes a distinct advance may be made and an entirely new outlook attained. This is a much more important vibration than most people are aware of, for every-

thing originating in the mind, those influences which bring
new thoughts, new ideas and progressive trends to the mind,
have the power to change the whole life and outlook of the
native.

The Sun in Adverse Aspect to Mercury.

This brings worries, anxieties, irritation and sensitiveness.
The native will feel unsettled and dissatisfied and will lose
the power to concentrate on his work and even the desire to
see it accomplished. It is a poor time for doing business,
especially if it entails buying, selling or dealing with agents.
Care should be taken in all things, especially in matters that
have to do with correspondence, writings, signing papers or
in handling documents. If other influences agree, the native
will be talked about, or else will talk too much himself and
much mischief may be done. Agreements will be unsatisfactory, and contracts also, and there will be unsatisfactory
relations with those who are connected with the native in
such matters. Any explanations or discussions will be more
or less futile and will only tend to place the native in a worse
position. It is best to keep silence as far as possible and
work on the plan that "least said is soonest mended".

Sun in Good Aspect to Jupiter.

This, of course, is the best influence there is for general
prosperity and advancement. The Sun with Venus marks
the happiest period in life, but this marks the most important
in the way of prosperity, good health and good fortune
for the native. All these will he receive while the door is
opened by this benefic vibration. It is a time when there
may be gains through speculations and investments, when
journeys for business may be undertaken with promise of
excellent results and when all business affairs should go well
with the native. Jupiter is the planet that brings actual money,
and the gains are substantial and quite tangible. With Venus
the benefits are more in the way of love, friendship and pleasures; but Jupiter can bring all these things, and more, and is
stronger for material gains than Venus. To women this influence frequently brings a man into the life, either as a husband
or as an influential friend, who may prove of great value

throughout life. Jupiter brings this advantage with his blessings—that as far as the nativity will allow, his gifts are permanent, and whatever advantages he offers may become permanent if he is able to make the proper use of them when the opportunities are offered. The period during which the Sun makes a good aspect to Jupiter, particularly if it should be the trine, stands out as a special period in the life, and no time ever quite comes up to this one for opportunities, favors, gains and advancement. This is a good time to travel, to push one's affairs, have dealings with foreign countries and to enter into philosophical, religious and legal affairs.

The Sun in Adverse Aspect to Jupiter.

This brings financial difficulties and losses and an unfavorable time generally, though, as with the other benefic, Venus, it can never bring such disasters as some of the other planets. There are times when it will bring a death or separation, and such separations are just as likely to be permanent as are the benefits, so that trouble between friends, families or relations tending towards separations should be carefully avoided, if possible, for it will be hard to unite the bonds when once they are broken through this vibration. It is not a suitable time to handle much money. Whatever the native may have should be securely placed and not used for investments, speculation or lending. Expenses are often heavier than usual; losses, extravagance and waste more easily incurred, and the period should be used by those who are going through it as an opportunity to learn economy, prudence and balance as related to all financial matters.

The Sun in Good Aspect to Saturn.

It is not unusual for the aspects of Saturn to show no definite good because, his nature being to slow up and solidify, the effects will generally be more along that line than any other, and it almost seems, at times, as though he brought disaster instead of gain. But later the native finds that everything is working out slowly, but surely, and that all he has to do is to hold fast and settle himself as the opportunities afford. When the Sun is in good aspect to Saturn, greater responsibilities will be placed upon the native. He will assume a better position, gained through the respect and confidence of others, and this makes it easier for him to accomplish even more while his honor and reputation are at their best. Working along the right lines at such a time and doing all that is necessary to strengthen his position, as well as character, he will find himself gaining ground and becoming a very substantial part of the community in which he finds himself. It is under such influences as this that, to those whose nativities will allow, there come opportunities for governmental positions, for some public work, or added prestige in the political world. These are the best vibrations for getting settled in the world in a firm position where increasing advantages are clearly seen if one is willing to hold on and work for the future in a steady, systematic manner. Money should be placed in sound investments; friends should be sought among those who are older, or who hold responsible positions, and the advice taken of those who have a reputation for sound judgment and good principles. Working in such a manner along every path in life, and on every plane, the native will find himself growing internally stronger, with greater resistance against change and unrest, and an increasing respect from his fellow men. Such is the manner in which he may become a substantial citizen of his country.

The Sun in Conjunction, Parallel or Adverse Aspect to Saturn.

The conditions change very greatly from that of the good aspects to Saturn, for everything will work out more or less to the misfortune of the native. Nothing will go right, and for the most part will not go at all, because it is through such vibrations as this that Saturn gets in his hardest lessons and withholds everything from the native, seeming to balk him at every turn. To start with, his health and spirits will be depressed, and he will not have so much energy or vitality to fight his way. There will be opposition, difficulties, delays and disappointments at every turn, so that there will be times, when other planets add their influence, that it will seem as if there is no way to turn and the whole world is against him. Very much greater care will be required in all dealings with other people. There will be fewer opportunities and those will be hard to make use of. There will be many conditions, chiefly domestic, that will cause worry and anxiety and, in any case, the native will be much more inclined to worry than usual. Everything will look dark to him and all ambition may be knocked out of him for the time being. Under such mental conditions it will be easy for any bodily complaint he may have to become chronic, and for that reason he should use his best efforts to keep from sinking into the sad and despondent state that will allow such disorders to get too strong a hold upon him. It is usually these influences that cause people to commit suicide because of insomnia, a long sickness, or through apparent hopelessness. If these people knew what the influences were and that when they begin to pass away they would have a very different viewpoint, they might be able to hold on until things again looked brighter. In many respects the aspects of the Sun to Saturn, good and bad, are the most important, and careful thought on this subject will soon reveal to the student why, and how. This is worthy of considerable study and investigation, for we are all strongly Saturnine and all our hardest and most important lessons come through the vibrations of this stern teacher.

The Sun in Good Aspect to Uranus.

Whereas Saturn takes things slowly and calmly, Uranus acts with suddenness, and always in some unexpected manner. Nothing goes the way one would expect, no conventions are followed, and all affairs take on an original and unique aspect. This is a very wonderful influence to live through, for it offers great scope, especially on the higher planes of thought and intuition. Romance frequently comes into the life under such vibrations and, in a woman's horoscope, will bring marriage, an unusual love affair or some quite extraordinary experience that has to do with friendships and affections. Sudden gains will often come; important changes may be made, long journeys taken, and all sorts of new and original plans and ideas formulated. This is a time when investigators, historians, archeologists and those interested in antiques may have big "finds" and when their labors will meet with just rewards.

Particularly, however, is it a good time to study occultism, to increase the intuition and to work along new, inventive and constructive lines.

The Sun in Conjunction, Parallel or Adverse Aspect to Uranus.

The conjunction and parallel are not wholly evil, but may easily become so in the case of those who are not well governed or self-controlled. In a favorable chart, especially where the Sun and Uranus are favorable towards one another, much progress may be made on the higher planes and most of the benefits of the good aspects may also be experienced, but for the most part it is a rather dangerous influence and will tend to cause very erratic actions and great irritability. The temper becomes queer and uncertain, while all the actions will be tinged with a certain lawlessness and unconventionality. It makes this a very unfavorable time for changes, for starting new undertakings or for travel, especially long journeys or any move through which radical changes in the life are made. It is most probable, however, that the influence will force the native to make changes, to cause some upheaval in the life and to upset its routine completely. One can depend upon nothing turning out as might be expected; nothing runs true to form, and most divorces and sudden separations come about through such influences of Uranus, while marriages, or any kind of partnerships, contracted while there is an adverse aspect of the Sun to Uranus will most certainly have a disastrous ending.

The Sun in Good Aspect to Neptune.

There are many people who make but little response to the vibrations of Neptune, excepting on the material plane where his action is not very strong at any time. To such persons this influence may bring prosperity financially, or some piece of "good luck," and is good for dealings in oil or liquids of any kind. It brings pleasures and much happiness and keener feelings of joyousness. But to those who are more spiritually inclined it will bring all this and more, for there will be exaltation, inspiration and enlightenment on the higher planes; quite possibly some remarkable vision or psychic experience. It increases the love of beauty and its appreciation and gives new inspiration along the lines of their particular interests to those who are sensitive, artistic and temperamental.

The Sun in Conjunction or Parallel to Neptune.

This may be entirely good in some cases and distinctly evil in others. It is a mystical influence and one which is difficult to delineate, as each person has a different reaction. Certainly, life will not run along in a smooth or easy manner, especially on the lower planes of action, and the tendency will be for one's affairs, as well as one's own mental processes, to become confused and not clearly defined.

The Sun in Adverse Aspect to Neptune.

This undoubtedly brings chaos into the life. Mental confusion is rarely absent and it is hard for the native to see clearly what is the best thing to do and then to be able to keep to the decision that he may make. Everything becomes more involved and there is certain to be some treachery or underhanded work against the native. If his chart should show him capable of such actions himself, it might be very easy for him to stoop to such things. In fact, there may be times when even those who have never before been guilty of such actions will allow themselves, under the confusion and chaos of mind which this may bring, to be guilty of deceit or fraud, or to be drawn into schemes which are not strictly moral or legitimate. Those who understand and realize what the vibrations are can withstand their subtle influences much better and are not so likely to fall prey to those who would deceive them; nor will they be so likely to do the dishonorable thing themselves. It may be frequently found that suicides, weird acts, unaccountable murders, and offenses that seem to have no particular motives are committed by those who are laboring under these most difficult vibrations.

CHAPTER 10.

ASPECTS BY THE PROGRESSION OF THE PLANETS.

MARS.

Mars in Good Aspect to Venus.

This is very stimulating, especially to the feelings and emotions. It causes strong attractions, much pleasure in the society of others and some very active friendships. It causes greater intensity of emotions and one is likely to show more "temperament" and expansion in feeling than usual. It is the kind of influence that can bring much happiness and buoyancy, but even the good aspects call for discretion and moderation in those things in which feelings and affections play any part.

Mars in Conjunction with Venus.

This is a questionable influence. For those who have their lower nature well in control it may be exceedingly good and give a new impetus and outlet for their love natures. But to those who are already amorous, there is grave danger of going to extremes and of acting indiscreetly and in a way that will react harmfully to both themselves and others.

Mars in Adverse Aspect to Venus.

The greatest care should be taken at such a time as this. Uncontrolled love and passions arise from this vibration, while there will be more or less continuous battle within the individual himself, a struggle for mastery between the higher and lower love natures. There will be opposition from those who are not in sympathy, disappointments through those on whom he pins his faith, and many temptations in the directions in which the desire nature is strongest. Discretion should be the watchword of those who have to go through this test, and on no account should unions be formed, or marriages contracted, while the aspect is in progress. Especially should all warnings be observed at such times, as there are other influences to excite this one into greater action.

(97)

Mars in Good Aspect to Mercury.

This indicates a quickening of all the mental faculties, for, Mars being the planet of action and Mercury the planet ruling the mind, the result should be especially gratifying, thus making it a good time for all mental work, for planning new lines of action and for all matters in which writings, correspondence and lecturing are concerned. The brain will act more quickly and also be more accurate. It is especially good for those who work with figures, or who are employed at stenographic work, for they will have greater speed and skill, as well as accuracy. The whole nature should be keener and more alert and the native will be better able to handle what comes his way. It adds enterprise and daring to the nature for the time being, and many people have been able to do things at such a time that would have been impossible before or afterward.

Mars in Conjunction or Parallel to Mercury.

This is not wholly evil, but is a rather difficult vibration, especially for those who have much of the Mars nature already active. It tends to bring too much impulse and rashness. The speech is usually too free, and, unless restrained, much mischief and trouble may ensue. Mentally it is very good, for it adds keenness, alertness, buoyancy and enterprise, and, so long as the individual is able to hold himself in check and keep poised, the results will be very gratifying.

Mars in Adverse Aspect to Mercury.

Scandal, ill repute, backbiting, too much talk, arguing and quarreling—all these things, or some of them, will be in evidence, and the greatest care will be needed if the native would avoid getting into some serious trouble. This is not the time to work on important documents, sign papers or agreements, or to write anything that might, in any way whatever, be used against one. In every way possible the honor should be guarded. It is an unfavorable time for travel, making any changes or for short journeys. Matters connected with books, publications, writings, lectures, etc., should be delayed or carefully handled while this influence is in operation.

Mars in Good Aspect to Jupiter.

We have two very strong forces here and great good may result from the contact. It gives an increase in magnetic power and the native may become so enthusiastic and so imbued with the excellence of some scheme that he will be able to influence many to his cause. It is usually a good influence for money making, and thus is a favorable time for investments, taking chances and for pushing affairs in any direction that seems good to him. Jupiter is philanthropic, and Mars being so forceful, it will give fresh impulse and new plans to those who are responding to that phase of Jupiter's activities. The emotions may be raised to a higher plane and all the feelings be nobler, more expansive and raised to a higher level. Enterprises and undertakings of any kind may be pushed forward and made more successful than if handled at any other time and so long as the native does not go to excess in anything, there is no limit to what he may accomplish. But with two such strong planets, and both of them fiery and impulsive in nature, there is always the danger of excess and of getting beyond control. Therefore this must always be considered before important matters are launched too far in any one direction.

Mars in Conjunction, Parallel or Bad Aspect to Jupiter.

The finances are in considerable danger during such a period, as Mars is adversely aspecting Jupiter. Since the aspect may last a considerable time (a period of several years), preparations should be made beforehand in order to get through this time with as little activity in money matters as possible. Waste, extravagance, poor judgment and indiscretion are all brought about by such a configuration. Troubles may be threatened from many directions, but if the lesson is being rightly learned, there will not be the same need to worry, for much will rest with the individual himself as to how this will work out. All legal matters should be avoided if possible, though it is quite often the case that the bad aspect of Mars to Jupiter will involve the native in spite of himself, and rarely is it, unless the nativity is particularly fortunate, that he will come out on the right side. Even though

he should get judgment in his favor, the expenses and annoyances would be great and there would be little real satisfaction. Excesses and extravagances of any kind should be
strictly avoided and a good deal of care will be required in
the matter of diet, for the system will tend to become overheated and the blood to be impure. Moderation, therefore,
in all things is called for—in living, food, drink, pleasures and
in finances. Only by such observances will the native be able
to get through this trying period without some disasters.
The conjunction and parallel will not be so evil as the other
aspects.

Mars in Good Aspect to Saturn.

This is another strong vibration, as, in fact, are all the
aspects of Mars, especially to the major planets, Jupiter,
Saturn, Uranus and Neptune, for Mars impels the great force
of these important planets into action, and unless the actions
are well controlled, there might be very serious trouble. But,
of course, the good aspects give one excellent chances to make
great progress, because the very force which Mars gives sends
one such a long way in whatever direction the impetus
may be and good aspects should give one the right start.
Saturn with Mars makes for steadiness, diplomacy and poise,
and usually there is greater skill in the management of one's
affairs. The native will be as enterprising as when Mars is
with Mercury or Jupiter, but he will have better judgment
and a better understanding in every way, because he will be
willing to look ahead and work for far-reaching plans. This
contact often brings the opportunity to rise through the recognition of one's ability and skill, especially in management,
and every effort should be made at such a time to plan and
carry out systematically any good ideas that might bring one
the favor of those in high places.

Mars in Conjunction, Parallel or Adverse Aspect to Saturn.

This will have the effect of dulling the vim and enterprise
of Mars so that there will be some depression that is not
usual. To those who are easily depressed it causes a peculiar
despondency and quick resentment towards those who do not
act in accordance with the native's own ideas; while those

who are too buoyant find in this a steadying influence which at times works quite to their benefit. If one is naturally resentful and bad tempered, the tendency is increased, and if other influences are also bad, events will occur to cause much trouble, and the ungoverned temper may lead to many unwise actions, lawlessness, violence, murder and all sorts of regrettable things, which would result in loss of character, ill repute and disgrace. A strongly Saturnine person will feel this much more than a Mars person and everything should be done to prevent too ready a response to this very evil vibration.

Mars in Good Aspect to Uranus.

This brings a strong magnetic force and all those who come under the influence will be more attractive in every way. There should be greater mental energy, more constructive thought and more ingenuity and originality in anything that one might attempt to do. It is under such an aspect as this that one can accomplish a great deal more than usual. There will be energy of body and mind, vitality, buoyancy and skill. A good deal of daring may also go with this, more so even than when Mars makes aspects to Jupiter, and the results will be more worthwhile, bigger, broader and far-reaching. It is a very fine influence for work on the higher planes and, if the other vibrations agree, there will be nothing to stop the native from making very marked progress. He may express such things as will astonish people, himself included, and will find within himself qualities he never before suspected.

Mars in Conjunction, Parallel or Bad Aspect to Uranus.

These aspects will bring a time when much care should be taken in every way. If the native is naturally rather weak mentally, or lacking in balance, it may produce a state anywhere from queerness to insanity and, for all persons, there is the tendency to do unusual things, to be more temperamental, erratic and less sure of themselves and their future actions. All through such a period caution and poise should be the watchwords. The nervous tension will be greater, for there will be many trying conditions to pass through and events will happen with such suddenness and uncertainty as to keep one continually on edge. Thus it is easy to see how it might affect those who are naturally in a nervous state. Queer accidents may occur, either through rashness or carelessness, or through handling electrical appliances.

Mars in Good Aspect to Neptune.

There is less direct benefit from this than from any other of the Mars aspects, owing to the queer influence of Neptune and the natural inharmony of the two planets. Of course, it will act somewhere and there will be some definite results on the material plane, but they will not be so easily traced or outstanding as those of the other planets. It is good for travel, for making changes, for money making, if other influences agree, and there will be a certain amount of "good luck" or good fortune from some unexpected quarter. Possibly it is more beneficial to those who write or who work along imaginative and creative lines where new ideas and inspiration are a necessity, as this will bring such things to those who are receptive. But there is danger, in all aspects of Mars to Neptune, of an undercurrent of secrecy or subtlety, though this will not show as a detriment to those who are naturally open and candid.

Mars in Conjunction, Parallel or Adverse Aspect to Neptune.

Some very serious harm may come to the native who has this configuration, especially if there are other indications either in the Natal or Progressed Chart. It is a time when great care should be taken against conspiracy, theft, treachery and subtle menacings. The reaction may be similar to that of Mars and Uranus and cause mental unbalance. It is a time when all things should be taken quietly and with as little excitement as possible. The emotions and feelings should be held in check and all drugs, narcotics and alcoholic stimulants should be left severely alone. The square is much the worst aspect and the opposition next, but all aspects of Mars to Neptune, even the good ones, tend towards a certain mental reaction that is not good excepting to those who are unusually well balanced or who are students along higher lines of thought and philosophy.

VENUS.

Venus in Good Aspect to Mercury.

In this case the conjunction is very good and should have a very decided effect upon the mind and the mental attitude generally. The native will be more cheerful and contented, because these are the qualities of Venus, and when added to the mental activities they help to alter the outlook on life considerably. He will lean more towards art and the beautiful in life, while pleasures, music and fun will all have more appeal. It always brings a more buoyant period and opportunity for expression in the brighter moods and fancies. It tends towards greater advantages and opportunities socially; brings new friends, more love and affection, or more demonstration of them, and is always a time when one can associate with friends and acquaintances with greater freedom and pleasure. It is a good time for making pleasant changes, for short trips of a social nature, for benefits through relatives, or through secretarial work, agencies or teaching.

Venus in Adverse Aspect to Mercury.

No aspect between two such planets as this can ever be very harmful, but it may bring trouble through the things already spoken of and it is a time when a good deal of care should be taken in speech and in dealings with those who are not truly friendly and interested. As with all aspects of Mercury, care should be taken in matters connected with writings, correspondence and signatures.

Venus in Good Aspect to Jupiter.

In this case, also, the parallel and conjunction are both good. But, strange as it may seem, the coming together of the two benefics in this way is not always the best thing, because there is an overload of the benefic, and therefore a liability to excess of some kind. It is better when this direction comes in with some adverse ones, for then it helps greatly to balance things and to give more buoyancy to an otherwise trying period. This aspect, of course, brings many friends, too many pleasures, possibly, and a good deal of happiness, joyousness and prosperity along any lines that are open. And, as always with the vibrations of Jupiter, there is tendency towards spiritual uplift, so if this line is chosen in preference to the more material, much greater benefits and progress may be made.

Venus in Adverse Aspect to Jupiter.

The same thing applies here as with Venus and Mercury. Nothing definitely evil can come from even the cross vibrations of these benefics. It may tend towards a financial loss of some kind or to disturbances in the home or with religious people and, coming with a number of other adverse influences, could help towards a loss of friendships, and cause considerable sorrow in those directions in which the affections are involved. It could also cause disappointment in one's immediate hopes and wishes, but little result is likely to ensue if it comes with otherwise good directions, or during a year when the Moon makes a series of good aspects in her progression.

Venus in Good Aspect to Saturn.

When Saturn, strong, grave and decorous, keeps company with Venus, the love planet, he will naturally tend to subdue the emotions and give quietness and strength to the affections. It is good for bringing about permanent friendships and love ties and makes for better relationships with older people or those who are quiet and staid in their manner. In restraining the feelings he does not repress them as in bad aspects, but gives them strength and endurance. Therefore, love affairs and friendships that are contracted under such a direction as this prove lasting and substantial, though they may lack the fire and sentimentality of affairs contracted under the Mars-Venus vibrations. Illustrating this influence still further, we find that when the Venus of one person's chart falls in conjunction, or good aspect, with the Saturn of another person's chart, there is a strong and deep affection that is permanent in its nature, though rarely of a demonstrative character. The reverse is also true; the bad aspects of these two in the respective charts will cause perpetual coldness, misunderstanding and sorrow.

Venus in Conjunction, Parallel or Adverse Aspect to Saturn.

The conjunction and parallel are not distinctly evil, but only so when other influences are in accord. In which case it brings a most unfavorable time for forming any ties, for marriage or friendships, as there is every promise of great disappointment through death or misunderstandings, or through interfering friends or relatives. Not only will it affect those things in which the affections and emotions are involved, but it will frequently bring about financial losses, either through lack of sympathy and understanding of others, or through one's own carelessness and indifference; or through a depressed state of mind which prevents clear thinking and quick action. It can bring a very trying time in every respect and, where it affects the feelings and emotions, can bring a condition of sadness, remorse, regret or depression that is very hard to combat.

Venus in Good Aspect to Uranus.

This brings the unexpected in regard to one's friendships and relations with other people. It brings a certain amount of success—financial, business or professional—but has most to do with those affairs in which the native is bound to others by ties of attraction or affection. Many surprises await those who have this direction in their chart and they will be surprises of a pleasant, happy nature which will bring about an altered state of affairs and some entirely new conditions. This is a time when the magnetic currents are stronger than usual and when one is attracted to, or attracts, others in strange and romantic ways. Even ordinary meetings with people will take on an air of romance or unusualness and life will lose much of its drabness and everyday air. To those who are naturally susceptible it is not quite so good, because they are liable to be too easily affected by others and to be too free with their love and emotions. But to the naturally conservative person it brings a greater interest in life and in the lives of other people, and to those of a still more elevated turn of mind it brings new interests in occult subjects and new friendships with those who also are interested in these things.

Venus in Conjunction, Parallel or Adverse Aspect to Uranus.

This causes much trouble in the life of the native and never passes without bringing about many important events and experiences. The parallel is not so definite in its action, and the semi-square and other weak aspects are not really important, but the conjunction, square and opposition always have a great effect and never fail to bring separation, estrangement or great sorrow that will much affect the future conditions. It brings strange and unusual attractions, and just as suddenly dissolves them. It brings people into the native's life in some unexpected manner and then estranges them just as quickly. There is nothing certain or well defined, and all things that have to do with the feelings and emotions will be strained and uncertain. The native will be at "outs" with himself, more uncertain in temper and in feelings, and will not know his own mind in regard to his feelings and relationships with others. If the nativity suggests it, there is danger of some scandal or notoriety which will seriously affect the character and it is therefore very essential that one should be more than usually careful and circumspect during such a period so as not to precipitate such matters. Discretion should be the watchword under these conditions.

Venus in Good Aspect to Neptune.

This brings about a very delightful state of mind to those who are able to respond to any extent to the vibrations of the mighty Neptune. It gives exaltation and peace with an understanding of the mysteries of life according to the development of the native. Beautiful friendships may be made at such a time; friendships quite out of the ordinary, and perhaps with little love of the ordinary kind in them, and certainly little of the sex attraction. All emotions are raised to a higher plane, and for those who are interested in art or music there is greater understanding and inspiration; they are able to work in delight and in buoyancy and with true art and expression. It is the best time for all expressions of feelings and emotions, because they will be freer from sensualism and crudeness than at any other time. Such an influence as this can save a person from great harm, and many difficulties, in what could otherwise be a year of real danger or problems. It is also good for investments and finances in the ordinary way, but those who are wise will seek expression on the higher planes, where they will get so much more that is worth while and permanent.

Venus in Parallel, Conjunction or Adverse Aspect to Neptune.

As usual, the conjunction and parallel are not wholly evil, for much will depend upon the natal aspects and the other influences operating at the same time. But they can rarely be wholly good, because we are not able to get sufficiently in harmony with Neptune for that. As with all Venus aspects, this will have to do with attachments, friendships or love affairs, and those coming through unfavorable Neptunian vibrations tend to have something abnormally sensual about them and not wholly pure or clean. The final results may be those of purification, but it will be through experience and temptations. It brings about peculiar attachments and love experiences and the magnetic influences during this time will be strange and unwholesome. There is great danger of scandal, ill repute and gossip; while love affairs of an earnest and true character will be broken through the treachery and falseness of others. Great care should be taken at such a time as this not only in these matters but also in finances and the things that are ruled by Venus or Neptune in the Radical Chart.

MERCURY.

Mercury in Good Aspect to Jupiter.

The good aspects of Mercury to Jupiter have a very good influence upon the mind, and are uplifting and buoyant. They help to clear the path for action, expand the consciousness and raise the whole tone of thought to a higher level. There is a decided effect upon the judgment, giving balance of mind, clearer vision and the ability to plan in the best possible manner. Jupiter being the planet that rules religion, philosophy and the higher sciences, and Mercury being the mental planet, it is certain to excite to action whatever of these lines are open. It is particularly good for all matters relating to litigation, for it helps the native in his judgment and also gives him good fortune in such matters. Lawyers and clergymen greatly benefit by this direction and all people are likely to benefit financially in some way, but chiefly in those things already mentioned, as well as through agreements, contracts and investments. The conjunction and parallel are wholly good.

Mercury in Adverse Aspect to Jupiter.

Now, instead of the native having good judgment and a fine sense of proportion, which obtained under the good directions, he will be liable to serious errors. The mind will not be clear nor at ease and there will be a lack of balance and steadiness. He will be more restless and unsettled and less discreet. All litigation should be avoided if possible, but with such an aspect as the square or opposition of Mercury to Jupiter the native is liable to be involved in it regardless of his own wishes or desires. This is a time when he must be unusually careful about signing contracts or seeking alliances with other people. Correspondence should be carefully considered. It will not do to place too much trust in other people and on no account should loans be made or asked for. It is easy to stretch the truth under these vibrations and to view things in a wrong light. Often there will be too much optimism at first, followed by depression, anxiety and worry, so that it is best, at such a time, to deal as little as possible with outsiders and to keep to routine work, or whatever will not lead to any of the above difficulties. One's honor and reputation are often at stake when these vibrations are at play.

Mercury in Good Aspect to Saturn.

The good aspects of Venus to Saturn steady the emotions, and the good aspects of Mercury to Saturn steady the mind and make a person much more practical and level-headed. There is a greater earnestness and a keener desire to attend to the duties at hand, as well as a more concentrative ability for all mental work. This is an excellent time to bring out the best of one's mental powers, to start new studies, make far-reaching plans and to review one's life and experiences for the purpose of greater understanding. All writings and correspondence may be transacted to good purpose, and all dealings with others will be more satisfactory and the results more permanent and secure. Even in money matters and ordinary business, things will be better and there will be the ability to arrange affairs so that they are on a better basis both as to permanency and remuneration.

Mercury in Adverse Aspect to Saturn.

This includes the conjunction and parallel to a certain degree, although these two will often have a benefic effect in giving greater concentration and steadiness. To those who have too much Mars the conjunction may act with real benefit, making a better balance and adding thoughtfulness and care to this type, who need it most. But the general tendency of all these aspects is to depress the mind and to cause a slump of mental activity. There is aroused in the native suspicion, gloom, worry and distress, making him for the time a poor companion, poor in business dealings and a "wet blanket" in the home. Much trouble may come under this direction, chiefly through the native's own mental attitude, which is warped while the vibration is hitting him. Despondency, fret and worry will detract from his good judgment and it is no time for important dealings with others, especially where writings, correspondence and signing papers are concerned. It often happens, under this direction, that mail goes astray or is long delayed, that unpleasant news comes by mail or that one reads of things of a sorrowful and depressing nature.

Mercury in Good Aspect to Uranus.

This direction invariably brings some kind of travel, frequently long journeys by rail, and now that transportation by air is becoming so popular it will be more frequently in that way than any other. Of course the mental processes will undergo some change and there will be a greater interest in all things of an occult and metaphysical nature. It gives a new impetus to the mind; greater originality, quickness and constructive ability. One may write and do things at this time that they thought impossible before and every effort should be made to make real the hopes and wishes of their life. Many things are possible at such a time that have no chance in the ordinary course of affairs and particularly will this apply to all literary work, studies in occultism and to inventions and unusual constructive lines. The magnetic currents will be stronger, and, for those who go in for mental healing and teaching of psychology, there can be no better influence under which to work and advance their own interests. Expansion in all mental lines is possible and every effort should be made to make the most of this benefic influence. The conjunction and parallel in this instance may be almost entirely good, though with certain types the mind will be less stable and more erratic, and there will be a greater nervous tension. The less balanced the mind, the greater the tendency to a mental or nervous breakdown at such a time, but for those who work on the higher planes it means opportunity for growth and advancement and a general upliftment of thoughts and ideals.

Mercury in Adverse Aspect to Uranus.

This tends to make a person very erratic and uncertain both in mental processes and temper. One is liable to change his mind very frequently and to make foolish and disastrous changes because of his inability to hold his mind to a proper balance. Those who are naturally weak mentally may be thrown completely off their balance by this vibration and they may commit acts that no sane person would consider. It will intensify the condition of those who are naturally hysterical and cause an inclination that way in those who have shown no evidence of it before, unless great care and self-control is exercised. The results of this vibration can be very disastrous to those who have not practiced control of temper or emotions and they should be warned to hold themselves well in hand and keep down the nervous tension which is certain to be one of the reactions to this influence. Altogether it is a time when great care should be given in all directions, particularly to speech, writings and trading.

Mercury in Good Aspect to Neptune.

To those who can respond to the spiritual influence of Neptune this is a very fine aspect and will give inspiration, uplift, enlightenment and mental happiness. It is a particularly good influence for those who write imaginative stories and for those who have special talent along some artistic line. Now is the time to develop whatever of latent genius one may have. On the lower planes the aspect gives a pleasant outlook on life, a more humorous turn to the mind and brings fun, pleasure and friends. There will be experiences of a peculiar and unique nature with friends and nothing will seem quite so ordinary and commonplace as usual. It is a good time to travel, especially on the sea, and also to take long, imaginative flights of fancy, if one is able to use the results in any practical manner. On the whole, the conjunction and parallel are good, though they incline to make the native more sensitive and susceptible to the influence of others. The action is better for those who are working on the mental and creative planes than for those who are in business or engrossed in mundane affairs. The effect is inclined to be especially detrimental to those who have to mix with all kinds of people and go into all kinds of places and environments where the conditions are coarse and unrefined.

Mercury in Adverse Aspect to Neptune.

This inclines towards treachery, fraud and deceit, either on the part of the native or in action against him. At such a time there may be scandal, goods stolen and false witness given, and may be disappointment in people in whom one has trusted and depended. Trouble may come from directions difficult to trace and it is no time to deal with people in matters of buying, selling, trading or correspondence. This is a time when suspicion of others will be justifiable and when one should be extremely careful of those in whom one may confide. It makes an unfavorable time to travel, especially on the sea, and not a good time to make any changes which depend upon the decisions and advice of other people.

JUPITER.

The Directions of Jupiter.

Jupiter moves slowly and he does not often make any aspects other than those signified in the birth chart. He will, however, frequently culminate an aspect and hold it for many years and that period will be greatly colored by his influence. For instance, if he is making a good aspect to one of the lights, he will stand as a safeguard against any great adversity coming to the native, even though there may be, at the same time, some truly malefic directions from other sources. Nothing will be quite so bad and there will always be some way out provided by the good contact of this great benefic. But if the culminating aspect is an adverse one, then at times, when there are other adverse directions or powerful influences from the transiting planets that could awaken this influence into action, there will be losses, financial and otherwise, difficulties with superiors, loss of position and favor and severe reverses in speculations.

It is rarely that Saturn does more than complete a close aspect at birth and his aspects at this time color the whole life all the time and are always felt when there are similar directions or transits from other planets. He has greater power than any other planet to make a life unfortunate, and when he completes an adverse aspect by direction, especially if it is to one of the lights, he has the power to take as much as half of the benefits promised by any of the benefic directions.

Uranus and Neptune cannot move sufficiently in an ordinary life to be considered in the directions, but their influence is felt in the transits. Being so slow in motion, these transits have practically the same power as the directions of the other planets. The action of these transits is given elsewhere in this book.

CHAPTER 11.

PARALLELS.

Progressed Positions of the Planets.

The declinations of the progressed planets are really of much greater importance and significance than the declinations of the Natal Chart. These act in a similar manner to the conjunction and have a definite influence upon the native, though perhaps this influence is rather more on the subjective planes than is that of the conjunction. The parallels must be within one degree of orb before they can be considered as having any definite influence, though if (as so frequently happens) the planet is passing from the parallel of another planet's radical place to the progressed declination of the same planet, or vice versa, even though there may be several degrees between, there will remain a continuous influence, though not so strongly defined, and getting more powerful again as the planet draws closer to the next parallel. This applies to all aspects unless there is a distance of more than a few degrees between.

Take, for example, the Sun going towards a square of Saturn; the Sun being in four degrees of Pisces in the progressed, and Saturn in five degrees of Gemini in the nativity, and progressed to seven degrees of Gemini at the particular period. The Sun, then, is just in orb of the square of the radical Saturn, being exact at five degrees, but instead of the vibrations ceasing when the Sun gets a degree past that square, it will carry over to the eighth or ninth degree, depending upon how far Saturn has moved by the time the Sun progresses to Saturn's progressed place. Of course, in the intervening time from the Sun's progress from the radical to the progressed Saturn, the vibrations will not be so strong as when the aspects are exact, unless some other influence of a similar nature occur to excite this particular one into action. If, however, the Sun were making a similar aspect to a quicker moving planet such as Mercury, and Mercury had progressed a whole sign from his radical place, then the effects of the Sun's aspect would not be carried over even if the progres-

sions brought the opportunity for him to arrive at the aspect
to Mercury's progressed position.

The parallels have greater strength if both planets have the
same direction as well as the same declination; that is, if both
are north, or both south, of the Equator.   When one planet
is parallel to another and is at the same time making an aspect
to that planet, either in the Radical or the Progressed Chart,
the parallel acts according to the nature of the aspect, simply
increasing its strength, whether it be good or bad, but in the
Progressed Chart it will not work so positively if it is counter
to anything in the Radical Chart.   Let us say the Sun is sextile to Saturn in the nativity and then progresses to a square
of Saturn, at the same time coming into parallel with the
same planet.   The planet would awaken the vibrations of the
natal sextile and the square would not then be so evil as if
the parallel were not there, on guard, as it were, to keep the
promise of the benefits of the nativity.   The reverse would,
of course, also be true; the good progressed aspect would
have less effect if a parallel excited an adverse aspect in the
Radical Chart.

Parallels of the Progressed Moon.

These are found in the same way as the Moon's longitude
for any given month and in delineating have, as has already
been given, much the same effect as the conjunctions of the
Moon to any other planet.

The New Moon.

The New Moon acts in a different manner to the transiting
Moon and more as the directions of the progressed Moon.
It frequently happens that the New Moon will make an aspect
to the same place for several months in succession, thus bringing the vibrations of that contact more definitely into play.
Each month the aspect will be different, beginning, for instance, with the conjunction and going to the semi-sextile,
then the sextile, the square and so on.   Much will depend upon
the nature of the planet aspected and its promise in the Radical
and Progressed Charts as to how the New Moon will affect it.

In one case where there was a continuous aspect of the New

Moon to Neptune, much treachery and intrigue was operating against the person in whose chart it fell, making things very uncomfortable for the time being, but since Neptune had only good aspects in the nativity, eventually everything turned out quite satisfactorily and no permanent harm was done. If it is the planet Venus that receives these aspects, it will bring friends, pleasant relations with women and children, or love affairs, more prominently into the life. If the chart promises well along these lines, the native will benefit very much each month that there is a good aspect and may even receive some benefit at the times of the evil aspects, and certainly will not feel the evil tendencies to any extent, so that, during the entire period, love affairs may proceed to a very satisfactory end. If, on the contrary, the radical or progressed positions of this planet were not good, then the effects of this would be reversed.

If the aspect were with Saturn, in favorable angles, then a steadying period would follow when new responsibilities would come, and when one would benefit through the advice and friendship of older people, and through all the things promised by the aspects and position of Saturn in the Radical and Progressed Charts. But if the ruling influence were adverse, then each month would bring fresh delays, difficulties, reverses, sickness, etc. Mercury aspected in this manner would bring greater activity to the mind, and to the work in which the native was employed—good or bad according to the conditions already stated. The culminating influence of the New Moon is not arbitrary, for much depends upon the excitement which comes from other planets operating at the same time. It may be that the day of the New Moon is the culminating point, or it may be at the time of the Full Moon. The latter is the more frequent, but results are determined by strength of position at the time. Sometimes the effect is so general that there appears to be no culminating point, and it may produce a prosperous period generally, or an unsettled period without any definite change; these, of course, depending upon the nature of the planet and the aspect made at the time.

We have known of a complete change of residence being made when the New Moon fell in conjunction with Mercury in the fourth house, and of a trip taken at the time of the New Moon conjunct Uranus close to the cusp of the fifth house, the house of pleasures, and ending close to the time of the Full Moon. Many interesting results have been obtained from a study of the New and Full Moons. These operating during any month when there are no directions from the progressed Moon will frequently be as strong in their effects as the progressed Moon herself. At the time when the New Moon is eclipsed, the effects are still stronger, though in no cases are the influences as strong when the aspects are made from succeedent or cadent houses as they are when they fall in angles. In this case the eclipsed Moon has a certain influence throughout the following year, making a more decided effect every three months when the Sun comes to the square or opposition of the point of the said New Moon.

The more influential the planet aspected, naturally the more powerful will the effect be. When the aspect is to the Sun, either radical or progressed, it will cause unsettled conditions and it will be a good time to make changes or to start new undertakings, or the reverse, according to the nature of the aspect and the inclination of the Sun. A chart made up on the day of the New Moon as though it were the native's own birthday (time, place, etc., of the real birth) and read in conjunction with the Radical Chart will often throw considerable light on the conditions for the month ahead. Also, a chart made up for the exact moment of the New Moon for the particular locality in which one is interested will reveal, in quite some detail, the conditions for that locality for the next twenty-eight days.

CHAPTER 12.

THE TRANSITS.

It is in this section of astrology that the real art of delineation is needed. It has already been stated that the Sun and Mercury are the most important planets in the Progressed Horoscope, but this is only from one point of view, for in the transiting planets lie the secrets of materialization of all events, both upon individuals and upon the world in general.

General influences and tendencies are to be found in the birth chart. The progressed planets indicate the periods in which certain of these become more active as well as indicating more specifically in which direction they will manifest, while the transits, also slightly affecting their direction, indicate with great precision precipitation of some of these.

The student must understand that transits will not affect every nativity alike, nor to the same extent. The nature and intensity of their influence will depend on the positions of the planets involved, both in the Radical and Progressed Charts. That is, if the transiting planets are in aspect in the radical horoscope, the influence will be strong; furthermore, if planets are in aspect by progression also, the influence will be still stronger and the events indicated by the progressed position will certainly be manifest at that time.

In one horoscope great importance should be placed on the transit of a particular planet, while in another its effect, though certain, is negligible. Every change in planetary positions has some influence upon the native and affects him upon one or all of the planes, even to the transit of such a quick-moving planet as the Moon. But, naturally, there are times when there will be a more decided influence than at others.

Suppose that by direction the Sun is making a good aspect to the Moon, or, if no aspects to the Moon, has, in general, good aspects, and the Moon, also by direction, during any particular month, makes a good aspect and no adverse ones, to one of the planets, then the transiting Moon will have little, or no decided, effect at the times that she passes the adverse angles to any of the planets. There will be a slight effect upon one of the planes, but it would take very careful watching to detect it.

All the good aspects will have a distinct benefit which may easily be noted. There are many people who have felt such good influences even during their sleep, especially when the Moon has touched such planets as Neptune or Uranus, more particularly the former. The reverse will also be true—when there are major afflictions, the transiting Moon's adverse aspects will be felt decidedly, and the good ones, very little. But, if the directions of the Sun are adverse, and the progressed Moon makes good aspects during any given month, then the transiting Moon will make itself felt in a different way. Taken without any other factors, the influences will be more equalized. The good aspects will be less beneficial and the evil ones less evil. But should there be some other transits at the same time from the major planets of a distinctly adverse nature, the evil of the Moon would be stronger; and if such major transits were good, then it would be the good lunar transits which would have the most power. This holds good with all the other planets, but is much more decided where the more powerful planets are concerned.

One more illustration will serve to make the point clear. We will take the planet Neptune as the opposite pole to the Moon. His transits are so powerful that they act in a very similar manner to directions, so that if the Sun were to make a trine to Neptune, by direction, and during some month the Moon, also by direction, made a good aspect to Neptune, then any good transits of Neptune would have a wonderful effect, and the period would be marvelously successful on all planes. But if, instead of the transit of Neptune being good, it was bad, then it would work in a different manner. The good aspect of the Sun to Neptune would make for unusual success, good fortune, riches and favors, and the Moon's influence would add to this. But if Neptune had a bad aspect to Mercury, by transit, then, while the other effects would still prevail, there would be some difficulties over correspondence, signing papers, confusion in regard to them, and in studies and all processes of the mind, while temperamentally the native would be oversensitive, more nervous and psychic and much more easily upset than would be otherwise natural.

This would be lessened or increased according to the angles of Neptune and Mercury at the time of birth. If both were well fortified, either by each other or by other planets, in the Radical Horoscope, this transit would be felt very much less.

When a planet transits the cusp of any house, and especially the angles, there is a marked event according to the nature of the house and sign. It should be remembered that the influence of the planet will be more or less marked all the time it is in that house, but its coming to the cusp marks a materializing point, just as an aspect to a planet will do, and each of these will affect the life according to the nature of the house, the aspect and the planet, as in all other cases.

There is also this to be remembered—that the dominance of the planets in the Natal Chart must be taken into account. If the Radical Chart shows that the native is easily angered and excited, all aspects of Mars to the cusps and to the planets will have an immediate effect upon the temper in one way or another. If the tendency is towards despondency, the aspects of Saturn will have a marked effect. If the native is naturally erratic, he will respond too readily to the vibrations of Uranus and, unless he is trying to keep himself well in hand, every time the aspects are evil, he will do some erratic thing or make some foolish change. We meet such people every day; they are continually stirred and wrought up over things to which a saner person would pay no heed. Extravagance strongly marked in the chart will bring quick-response from Jupiter, and the native will do well to watch the aspects; otherwise he will find himself continually engaging in extravagances, expenditures and speculations that will eventually be his undoing. By the indolent and amorously inclined person, the effects from Venus will be felt the most, and to those who are unsettled and changeable, every turn of the Moon will bring response.

We have in mind one case where a young man had heavy afflictions between Venus, Neptune and the Moon. This, among other things, gave him a weak and sensual nature, with a strong tendency to drink. A friend who was interested in him and anxious to get him out of this condition had us cast his Progressed Horoscope, giving the days when he would be most likely to fall. It was remarkable how this poor fellow responded to the influence of these three planets, but, by patience and watching, the friend was able to do much towards helping him pull himself together.

Those who have the mental planet, Mercury, strong in their charts and who are thus naturally studious will find that the influences of Mercury will give them fresh impetus and new ideas. We know one man who writes, but who is rarely able to do anything when Mercury is retrograde, or making bad aspects to his sensitive places. Thus it is that we find each person responding to different influences. The transit of the ruling planet is always very marked, especially when it is passing over the mid-heaven or ascendant, and will always bring a decided result, benefic or otherwise according to the nativity or the nature of any aspects that it may make at the same time. It is by this means that one is often able to rectify a chart where the exact time is not known.

To illustrate the effect of transits we will take our chart on Plate 1. The two outstanding things that we will consider for this discussion are a strong bent towards inventions and an extremely sensitive organism. Thus, all aspects and transits of Uranus bring a response, set the mind working upon new ideas and projects and bring new plans of invention and reform. But, whenever Mercury is hitting a sensitive point, he will be more nervous or sensitive in some way, according to the nature of the sign, aspect and house.

To illustrate still further, if the aspect were adverse to the ascendant, it would cause neuritis or some indisposition due to nerves, which would depend upon the nature of the ascendant; that is, if it were Aries, there would be a nervous headache, toothache, etc. If it were Cancer, it might be nervous indigestion, and so on. In this case the sign rising is Virgo; therefore, if the native were not careful of his diet, the tendency would be bowel trouble caused through a nervous condition and would express itself definitely through the sign that Mercury was in at the time of making the aspect, and through the nature of any other aspects he might be making at the same time. Thus, with Saturn it would be constipation, and with Mars or the Moon, diarrhoea. If Mercury were aspecting the second cusp, there would probably be nervousness or anxiety in regard to finances, especially those pertain-

ing to a partner, because the sign on that cusp is Libra. And
so on through all the various houses and signs.

There are many persons, having very afflicted charts, who
are hit by every passing influence and thus live a life of continual upheaval and adversity. There are others easily angered, very nervous, changeable and uncertain; so that there
is continually some planet making itself felt in their chart
and they are torn this way and that, almost without a let-up.
Others again are so phlegmatic and despondent that nothing
seems to awaken them or stir them out of their dismal and
unprogressive attitude. It must also be remembered that
transits do not always have the same importance. There are
times, with certain characters, when they will act in a remarkable manner, and other times when they will not be felt at
all, in a way that may be noted.

First of all must be considered the tendency of the Radical
Chart; then the directions for the year of the Sun and the
major planets; and finally the sign and house position of all
of them. It is the planets that are in angles at the time of
birth that bring the most noticeable events on the material
plane, for that cross, represented by the four angles, corresponds to the Earth and to this plane of manifestation, and
thus the planets therein are the fateful ones that bring to the
crystallization point those conditions which are to be met in
this incarnation. When a planet returns to a conjunction of
its own radical place in the chart it will tend to awaken all
that is promised by that planet through its position and aspects. If it is a so-called evil planet and has bad aspects,
one may expect a difficult time. And the benefics will bring
their good fortune at such a time. For instance, to those
whose charts are not heavily afflicted the birthday anniversary
always brings gifts, pleasures or special favors. The Sun
makes a complete revolution every year, the Moon once in
28 days, Mercury in 88 days, Venus in 224½ days, Mars in
1 year and 322 days, Jupiter in 12 years, Saturn in 39½ years,
Uranus in 84 years and Neptune in 165 years.

Transiting Planets Through the Houses.

The transits of Saturn, Uranus and Neptune, particularly
the latter two, over the ascendant and through the first house,

are exceedingly important, for being so slow in their movements they stay in one position for a considerable time and the effects are much like those of the progressed planets. Therefore, when these planets pass over the ascendant and at the same time make some adverse aspects—or even if they do not have any other aspects at all except this conjunction to the ascendant—conditions in the life of the native will be very strenuous and very frequently, in the case of elderly people, or those in poor health, they bring about death. Any planet aspecting the ascendant will bring about a change of some kind on some plane. The Sun, Venus and Jupiter will usually add to the weight of the physical body and give buoyancy to the mind; while Saturn, Mercury and Neptune tend to reduce the flesh and make one more nervous, sensitive and depressed. The action of the other planets in this respect is not so certain because the reaction is not always the same. A good deal will depend upon the signs they are in. For instance, Mars, in some charts, will give such an increase of bodily energy that it will be impossible to add to the weight; while Neptune could cause indolence and indulgence so that flesh could be put on rapidly. These delineations will apply also to a lesser extent when the planets make good or bad aspects to the ascendant from the other parts of the chart. As previously stated, it is when a planet comes exactly to the cusp of a house that it makes its presence most felt and it is often by this method that the exact moment of birth may be obtained.

THE FIRST HOUSE—WELL ASPECTED.

Moon.—Change, quick action, restlessness. All the foregoing planets move so rapidly that their effect is but little noticed unless specially watched. More particularly does this apply to the Moon, but frequently enough it will be the deciding influence in some particular event and will bring a thing to a head that otherwise might be delayed several hours or several days as the case might be. The New and Full Moon will have the same effect as is here mentioned, but will be much more potent and important, especially the New Moon, as will the influence of all the other planets if they come at the time of the New or Full Moon.

Mercury.—New ideas, possibly a change of some kind, an increased desire for literature, writings, etc.

Venus.—A fortunate time for holiday making, for social affairs, marriage, pleasures and music. Usually there comes an invitation, a gift, or some other expression of love and affection.

Sun.—All personal affairs are vitalized. Some good fortune or perhaps an opportunity. It is a good time to ask favors, or to seek promotion or advancement and to deal with superiors.

Mars.—Activity in all personal affairs, increased energy and ambition; increased vitality.

Jupiter.—Brings good health, increase in weight, vitality, more buoyant spirits and hopefulness, and very frequently some special offer or opportunity.

Saturn.—Will tend to steady the mind and slow up all operations; to bring new responsibilities, or a keener sense of responsibility, and an increase of patience and caution. He will often reduce weight and flesh and also cause some sickness or disability, even when well aspected.

Uranus.—Sudden changes, unexpected personal advantages, travel, higher trend of thought, surprises, marriage, breaking up of old ideas, habits or conditions and a complete change for the better in some particular direction.

Neptune.—This transit makes the native much more sensitive and psychic, and, if there are any mediumistic tendencies, these will be increased. There will be some secretiveness in one's personal affairs and peculiar conditions will arise to alter the trend of one's life. The line along which these things will work depends upon the sign that is on the ascendant.

THE FIRST HOUSE—AFFLICTED.

Moon.—Adverse changes, wounded feelings, increased sensitiveness and some indisposition, if in a female chart.

Mercury.—Quick changes in occupation or habits. An unfavorable journey, or difficulties or annoyances in connection with them. Nervousness and irritability.

Venus.—Difficulties with personal friends, in love affairs or pleasures. Some disappointment.

Sun.—Trouble with superiors. Controversies. Sickness through lowered vitality. Loss of honor or prestige.

Mars.—Anger, impulsiveness and danger of accidents. Headaches, feverish complaints, boils or trouble in that part of the body which is ruled by the ascending sign.

Jupiter.—Extravagance, or waste in health or habits, and an increase of pompousness and pride.

Saturn.—Ill health (all planets in bad aspect to the ascendant will tend to bring about ill health, and this planet more than any), depression, taciturnity, delays, annoyances and setbacks.

Uranus.—Unexpected changes of an unfavorable nature, breaking up of old habits and ties. This influence is very separative in its nature and erratic in its action. It is the unexpected that will happen with Uranus in this position and often changes will take place that will alter the whole tenor of a person's life.

Neptune.—Increased impressionability, sensuousness, moroseness, queer experiences and possibly queer dreams. There will be confusion, intrigue, treachery, and much trouble in ventures undertaken at this time.

THE SECOND HOUSE.

Moon.—Some changes in money matters for the better. Afflicted—Changes for the worse.

Mercury.—Financial gains through agencies, through handling contracts and through taking short journeys. When afflicted it is an unfavorable time for taking short journeys, especially if on business or with the object of collecting money. A time to be careful in all matters requiring signatures or promises. Hasty or indiscreet speech could result in direct loss of money.

Venus.—Gains through women and friends, through pleasures and things to do with food, sweet-stuffs and women's clothing. Afflicted—Loss through indulgences, laziness and carelessness.

Sun.—Gains through superiors, through influence and good position. Afflicted—Difficulties with men, employers or important personages, over finances. Loss of money if much afflicted at birth.

Mars.—Well aspected—Gains through one's own activity and enterprise. Afflicted—Loss through foolish impulses, poor judgment or quarrels.

Jupiter.—Financial gains, prosperity and success with speculations. Increase in financial prospects and new opportunities to make money. Afflicted—Waste, extravagance and loss.

Saturn.—Some opportunity to make money where there is responsibility; money will not be easy, but financial affairs may be placed upon a more substantial and permanent basis. Economy and prudence in money matters. Afflicted—Will restrict the income in some way; perhaps shut it off altogether, and also cause financial losses and difficulties.

Uranus.—Certainly will bring changes, unusual conditions in regard to finance, and opportunities for making money in unusual ways. Unexpected things will happen. Afflicted—There will still be changes, but they will be disastrous and disintegrating.

Neptune.—Gain, possibly through hospitals or institutions of some kind, or through some bubble scheme or obscure ways. Afflicted—Chaotic conditions in money matters, danger of fraud, uncertainty and possible disaster.

THE THIRD HOUSE.

Moon.—The Moon passing so quickly will not have much effect, but makes a good hour for starting on a journey or for making changes. If afflicted, best to wait till later in the day or till another day. The mind will be restless.

Mercury.—With Mercury in this position the mind is always more restless and active. It is rarely good for concentration and there is desire to do too many things at the same time, to change, to start new books, new ventures, and see new places.

Venus.—A peaceful state of mind, contented with conditions for the time being and very friendly terms with relations. Pleasant correspondence and invitations will be received and possibly there may be a short pleasure trip. Afflicted—The thoughts will be less pure; there will be longings for luxury and enjoyment and discontent with commonplace conditions.

Sun.—Advantages through any journey taken; a good time to make changes and to seek for position, especially if it is connected with teaching, stenography, salesmanship or anything coming under the rule of the third house. Afflicted—An adverse time for these affairs and for seeking interviews, especially with relatives.

Mars.—The mind will be more active and restless with increasing desires. Likely to be short trips and impulsive action. Afflicted—Short journeys will not be favorable; not a good time to write letters; danger of bad temper and quarrels, especially with or through relatives and neighbors. If very much afflicted, there may be an accident or operation to a brother or sister or some near relative.

Jupiter.—Excellent for seeking promotion or an increase in salary, if employed in third house affairs, or acting as go-between for anyone. Favorable outcome for any journey undertaken. Afflicted—Care should be taken to avoid being aggressive or too expansive, thereby causing offense. It could mean the loss of a position, or a break with relatives.

Saturn.—This position will steady the mind and give a greater attention to detail and to duty. Old incidents and letters will be referred to and there may be meetings with member of the family not seen for a long time, or those who are much older. Afflicted—Will bring a tendency to depression and sadness, disappointments through travel, or relatives, and in the occupation. Also delays in any planned journey or many difficulties in connection therewith.

Uranus.—This should stimulate the mind to higher lines of thought, to occult subjects and an interest in the unusual, curios and antiques. It is rarely that Uranus passes through this house without bringing a great deal of travel and unsettledness. Afflicted—There is trouble through these affairs; the native is more erratic and uncertain in temper and temperament and inclined to be irritable. Care should be taken to avoid controversies with others, particularly one's own family.

Neptune.—This is not a good place for Neptune, even if well aspected, unless in a very high type of chart, for he will tend to produce queer mental conditions, fears, anxieties, dreads, disturbing dreams and a restless state of mind generally. If there is much affliction, the native may become very morbid, even to the point of becoming mentally unbalanced.

THE FOURTH HOUSE.

Moon.—There may be some slight changes taking place in the home or home conditions; nothing of importance unless an excitement to some other more vital influence. Women frequently move their furniture around at such a time, and if the Moon makes good aspects to Venus or Saturn they get a tidy spell and clean up all the corners and dark places. If afflicted, they will do the reverse and neglect the things that ought to be done and be restless for a change from home conditions.

Mercury.—If well posited, this will be a good time for signing agreements or documents in regard to the home, real estate and property generally. It will be a good time to make changes, buy or sell a home, bring relatives into the home and to make journeys away from and back to one's place of residence. If afflicted, there will be need for care in all these things, especially in signing of any papers or documents connected with the home or other property, for the outcome will be very unsatisfactory and confused.

Venus.—This is an excellent position for Venus, as she will bring peace and pleasure into the home. A good time to invite people to visit, and also for buying or selling property. Afflicted—Will not affect the native very much, but may cause a disappointment or trouble with women members.

Sun.—The Sun in the fourth is very good for all matters that have to do with the home. It may bring important people to the home, or honor or promotion. Afflicted—Conditions during the month that the Sun is there will be unfavorable, and real estate, investments in property and mining should not be undertaken.

Mars.—There will be greater activity in the home and more ambition in that direction. As with the Moon, Mars frequently brings about changes owing to his being the natural ruler of the first house and of Aries. Afflicted—Danger of hasty moves or changes in the home which will end in trouble. An unfavorable time to deal in real estate, mining, and things pertaining to the Earth.

Jupiter.—Jupiter is always welcome in an angle, and in the fourth he brings better home conditions, a greater expansion in the home in some way, and an abundance of everything. This is the time when one should seek to settle permanently into congenial surroundings, for Jupiter always brings permanent benefits. The writer knows of one woman who had been in business for a great number of years, and who retired, but was uncertain as to where to locate herself and finally decided, just as Jupiter came to the cusp of the fourth house, upon a place that was exactly suited to her needs. She has remained there for a number of years and may stay in the same place until the end of her life. Jupiter in this house makes for sociability in the home, for better and more harmonious domestic conditions, and brings a better chance of present issues having a successful ending. If afflicted, there will be waste, extravagance or legal difficulties in connection with the home, property or investments.

Saturn.—Not so good in this position, unless particularly well aspected at birth, and also while passing through this house. The end of affairs started at this time will not be so satisfactory and will be delayed beyond a reasonable time. Saturn brings domestic troubles, sometimes deaths, or causes one to think about death, to prepare for death, to make wills, and to put one's affairs into order in case anything should happen. It is unfavorable for making changes, brings depressing and hampering influences, difficulties with one's father, or heavier responsibilities. Unless very well aspected, it makes everything in the home rather more depressing and heavy, but if Saturn is favorable in both the nativity and the Progressed Chart, everything will be quieter, more settled and reposeful. But it is rarely that one can expect definite improvement in affairs when Saturn is in an angle.

Uranus.—When Uranus reaches the fourth house there is certain to be some radical change in the home. It usually means a complete removal—sometimes to another town altogether. The changes come very suddenly and in an unexpected manner. Everything in connection with the home becomes more uncertain and unsettled. If the aspects are good, everything will turn out well, but if afflicted, it will be necessary to be unusually guarded so as not to be taken by surprise, for actions made in haste will surely be repented at leisure when Uranus is in question. When it has to do with the environment and home life, as the fourth house has, it means an upheaval at the root of one's affairs, and this is a very serious matter. It is at such a time that divorces frequently take place, or an estrangement in the home life, and such events always leave much to be regretted. If there are many planets in the radical fourth, it denotes a very critical time while Uranus is in this position, for each time he passes over one of these planets he brings a crisis into the life, and since he will probably retrograde back and forth over some of them, the whole seven years of his sojourn in this house will be very critical and bring about many changes, alterations, unsettled conditions and surprises.

Neptune.—As with all the other planets, Neptune is more forceful when in an angle and therefore has great significance when in this fourth house. The angles are the materializing points and precipitate the events on the material plane that are promised in the nativity, whenever any of the planets come to these positions with sufficient force to excite the promised things into action. Thus it sometimes comes about, and this was particularly noticeable in 1926, when the major planets Jupiter, Saturn and Neptune were square to one another, that more than one important planet will be transiting angles, in some particular nativity, at the same time. This, of course, brings about some very critical situations, not necessarily evil, but critical in the sense of bringing events to the materializing point and releasing stored up karma and experiences. Unless very well aspected, Neptune in this house tends to bring confusion into one's domestic affairs, to bring a cloud over the home, to make conditions more chaotic and uncertain and to bring some kind of deception or treachery into the home. It is very unwise to consider the purchase of a home, or property of any kind, while Neptune is in this position, unless the other influences are very promising. For even though Neptune is well aspected in the nativity, we cannot always raise our own vibrations sufficiently high to be harmonious enough to prevent adversities. In one nativity Neptune in the fourth brought about a fire which destroyed everything in a most unexpected and extraordinary manner. Of course there were other influences brought to bear to cause this, but it was primarily Neptune that brought about the

event. And then, immediately following, Neptune retrograded back and forth over the radical Moon in the fourth
house and caused all sorts of unsettled and annoying situations, some treachery, and continuous minor changes for the
year that this lasted. Afflicted—An afflicted Neptune in the
nativity will make home life and home conditions most trying. Events will probably occur that should be covered up,
and either make, or reveal, skeletons in the cupboard, and
perhaps also voluntarily, or by force, cause one to conceal
many things from the public.

THE FIFTH HOUSE.

Moon.—Not much change will be effected by the Moon in this
position, unless the native is a very high-strung, temperamental person; then the feelings may be overwrought.

Mercury.—Brings more seriousness in pleasures, a greater interest in reading and study and all mental things, while the
emotions will be less active. If afflicted, the native will be
more talkative, nervous and sensitive.

Venus.—This being the love planet, and the fifth house the
house of love affairs, pleasures and emotions, the vibrations
will be harmonious. Thus all these things will be more active
and beneficial, unless Venus is afflicted, and then it will make
for an excess in such matters; if very much afflicted, there
will be some immorality.

Sun.—The Sun is at home in this house and therefore his
passing will be good for the things that pertain thereto—
pleasures, theaters, children, speculations, and all the avenues
through which the emotions and affections are expressed.
Afflicted—Could bring some trouble or sorrow through, or
by, children, or through speculations.

Mars.—This acts upon the emotions and tends to give fire to
the passions. It will bring love affairs or violent attractions,
and increase the gambling instinct. Afflicted—There is danger
of quarrels and fits of passionate anger, and the desire to
take risks of various kinds, especially in gambling, may be
very marked.

Jupiter.—There is usually both the desire and the opportunity
for speculation when Jupiter enters the fifth house. There may
be gains through investments or undertaking new enterprises

with resulting good fortune. There should be more activities in pleasures, holiday making, and, in a woman's chart, there should certainly be a friendship with a man. If the woman is of marriageable age, there will be an attachment of a very joyful nature—beneficial, permanent and wholly satisfactory, if the nativity will allow. Afflicted—There will be an excess of emotion, unwise speculations and extravagances, some gambling and money wasted on women, or lost in some other foolish manner.

Saturn.—This acts in the reverse manner to Jupiter and, instead of bringing about attachments and love affairs, is more likely to break any that may be in progress, to make the native colder, less emotional and less responsive to the magnetism of others. Afflicted—It will bring disaster to love ties, coldness, callousness, hardness and stolidity according to the natural tendency of the chart. Sometimes it may be good, for it cools down the emotions and inclines the native to purity and chastity.

Uranus.—Sudden and unexpected gains through investments or speculations, and an interest in unusual lines of pleasure and hobbies. Violent and sudden attachments, love at first sight and all such unusual events in connection with the emotions. Afflicted—Very bad for love affairs and almost certain to produce estrangements or separations with those to whom one is attached. To those who have children there will be some unexpected trouble in connection with them.

Neptune.—Where Uranus always brings the unexpected, Neptune brings confusion; nothing will be so clearly defined or satisfactory when Neptune passes into the fifth house. It will be a poor time to start speculations because the judgment will be clouded, and when Neptune is afflicted there is danger of being defrauded or deceived.

THE SIXTH HOUSE.

Moon.—The few days that the Moon takes to pass through this house often brings an attack of indigestion, especially if there are any afflictions at the time, or in the nativity, and also tends to bring nervousness and irritability.

Mercury.—Well aspected—favorable for interviewing people, especially employers and employees. Also favorable for seeking medical advice and for seeking apartments and hotels. Good also for buying chickens, rabbits and other small farm stock. When afflicted it is adverse for these things and also adversely affects the health, especially of those who are nervous, for it tends directly to increase this malady, and indirectly others.

Venus.—Gives good health or, if there should be any sickness, there will always be the proper love, care and attention necessary, and a speedy recovery. It is a good time to seek work of any kind, to deal with servants and to employ them. Afflicted—Tends to bring about sickness, due to excess or overindulgence.

Sun.—The Sun in the sixth, if unafflicted, is very good, for it will benefit the health, add to the vitality and increase weight. It is also good in matters connected with inferiors and superiors in employment. Afflicted—The vitality will be decreased and work will become more of a burden during those thirty days than usual.

Mars.—There is a tendency to overwork when Mars enters the sixth house, which is the house of sickness, and this could bring about a breakdown through nervousness or high tension. If the aspects are good while Mars is in this position, it will be a good time to seek employment, start out along new lines and to push forward along whatever lines are open, provided caution and discretion are used. Afflicted—A bad time for all these things, and the native will probably spoil his chances for employment or progress by being too aggressive, or because he did not take time to plan and consider carefully his enterprises before launching out upon them.

Jupiter.—This is good for the health and most people gain in weight when Jupiter passes through this house. Good for seeking employment, changing work, dealing with servants, changing help, and generally securing the favor and appreciation of those who are working for one, or for whom one is working. Afflicted—The judgment will not be so good in any of these matters and prospects may be spoiled through overconfidence, overenthusiasm, or conceit, according to the nature of the afflictions.

Saturn.—Saturn always acts in the reverse manner to Jupiter. Therefore, instead of the health being better, it is likely to be poor. There will be a loss of vitality and, to those so inclined, attacks of indigestion or dyspepsia, so that greater care will be needed in diet than usual. It is a difficult position for those seeking employment, for there will be obstacles and delays, either because the business of prospective employers is poor, or because the native's own health will be unfit for the work. It will not be a good time for dealing with servants or those who are working under one. When Saturn is in good aspect, everything will be much better, though there will still be delays and obstacles in matters connected with employment, but eventually conditions will settle themselves more permanently, and responsibilities will come which will mean an advance in position. Afflicted—All the adverse predictions will be accentuated and there is certain to be some sickness which will be of long duration; or else some chronic ailment will arise out of the weakness to that part of the body attacked by the particular afflictions of Saturn.

Uranus.—Uranus coming to the sixth house is certain to bring, if the native is working for others, a change in employment, either in regard to the character of the work or the position of the native. A well-aspected Uranus will bring an improvement in the health by supplying more magnetism and vital energy, and the native may have greater power over those with whom he works. Afflicted— This will act in just the reverse manner and there will be continual trouble through sudden and unexpected quarrels, irritations, poor health from some obscure causes, and undoubtedly changes in employment which will be beyond the control of the native, and very much to his detriment.

Neptune.—If Neptune is well aspected he will not be felt much while in this house, though it is never a very good position for this planet, for he will tend to affect the health through psychic conditions. Care should always be taken to keep away from crowds, from spiritualistic seances, and all places where the air is likely to become vitiated. Afflicted—There will be treachery among those with whom one has to work. Servants will be deceitful. Employers will make promises that cannot be fulfilled, and those things connected with one's daily tasks will be confused and unsatisfactory.

THE SEVENTH HOUSE.

Moon.—This position could bring a change of partnerships, or some changes in the manner of cooperation, but is, of course, not important.

Mercury.—A time when contracts may be signed, hearings take place in connection with lawsuits, and when one is more likely to be active in signing papers and agreements. Afflicted—It will be unfavorable for these things and particularly should the signing of contracts be left to a more propitious time.

Venus.—This is a very good place for Venus. While the transiting Venus does not stay long in this position, yet it has time to bring about benefits through marriage, or even marriage itself, if the other conditions so promise, and helps to make all matters of litigation and association with others pleasant and profitable. Afflicted—Even then Venus can do very little harm, though rather more care, in all the matters mentioned, will be advisable.

Sun.—It is always beneficial when the Sun comes to an angle, for it brings benefits, chiefly business, and particularly through partners and corporations. Afflicted—If the Sun is much afflicted there will be loss of favor and prestige in the above matters.

Mars.—If Mars is well aspected, it brings activities in the way of partnerships, litigation, and matters that have to do with corporations and groups of people. It will sometimes bring about marriage or a business partnership, and, if so, it is done rather hurriedly, with lack of proper thought and arrangement. However, the activities should turn out well, for the native will have enough enterprise and courage to see the thing through in spite of the poor start. Afflicted—It is very bad for all the above-mentioned things. There is danger of quarrels and of lawsuits which will be very trying to the temper, while marriage conditions will be precarious and a dissolution easily brought about by anger, impatience and violent quarrels.

Jupiter.—When Jupiter is well aspected in the nativity this is particularly good, and one of the best times to marry. It is excellent, in fact, for partnerships and unions of all kinds, and brings opportunities to overcome one's open enemies. Afflicted—It is likely to bring trouble and loss through lawsuits, extravagance on the part of the partner, ill-advised actions and some affliction to the health.

Saturn.—This brings responsibilities in connection with other people, or brings one in contact with older persons, or those who are serious minded and stern. It should make unions still more binding, cement friendships and love ties and make for more settled conditions in connection with partners and coworkers. Afflicted—This is a very bad position for those who have Saturn afflicted in the nativity, for it brings coldness between husband and wife, builds up a barrier between them that is hard to break, and makes for misunderstanding and disappointments in all dealings with partners and those whose lives are in any way closely associated with that of the native. All litigation undertaken at this time will end unfavorably for the native, and there will be continual delays and obstacles in the way of progress. In many cases it greatly affects the health because this is the opposition point to the ascendant, and there are times when it causes falls or some other accidents. To those subject to rheumatism it brings renewed attacks.

Uranus.—Saturn, Uranus and Neptune move so slowly that they are a long time getting away from the opposition to the ascendant. Thus they have time, often, to seriously affect the health. Uranus in this position, even though he is not afflicted, will usually bring some nervous complaint such as neuritis, a nervous breakdown, an operation or some peculiar complaint that is difficult to diagnose. Apart from the health, Uranus in the seventh house will bring about a sudden marriage, if one is of marriageable age, or bring about a partnership or marriage union of some kind, even though there is no ceremony attached to it. Afflicted—This indicates broken bonds, the severing of marriage ties, or partnerships, and unexpected defeat in any lawsuits that may be on hand. There may be loss of friends, loss of lover, a good deal of ill feeling on the part of those whose work lies along the same lines, and new enemies will be made from unlooked-for quarters.

Neptune.—This position also, as with Uranus, tends to produce nervous disorders, due mainly, however, to queer fancies, a distorted imagination and suspicions, fears and anxieties about the partner, whether of marriage or business. When

Neptune is not afflicted there may be an unusual and unique friendship, or bond, which will help to counteract much of the ill effects upon the physical body.   Afflicted—Deception on the part of the marriage partner will come at such a time, if promised in the nativity, and it is under such influences that business partners prove to be fraudulent, run away with all the business funds, and, possibly, run away with the native's wife as well! Lawsuits will be lost through double-crossing, perjury, or deceit in some form.

THE EIGHTH HOUSE.

Moon.—The Moon in the eighth sometimes marks the day of a death, if one is promised in connection with the native. Otherwise little will result from this position, unless it be more dreams than usual.

Mercury.—This will tend to make the native more sensitive to vibrations from the astral plane and will also bring some unusual dreams or communications from the other planes. If well aspected, it may bring gain through partners, or matters where agreements or contracts are handled.   If afflicted —loss through these things.

Venus.—Also unimportant in this position, though some gains may come through death, or through one's husband or partner.   The same can be said of Jupiter in the eighth house in regard to these gains.   If the directions indicate danger to the native, the position of Venus in this house will serve as a protection, unless heavily afflicted.

Sun.—This helps in the partner's finances, especially if they have any dealings with important people or superiors.   If well aspected, much good may be derived in this way or through a legacy.   If afflicted, there will be difficulties or losses in these matters.

Mars.—Unless this position of Mars excites some directions into action it is not likely to have much effect. But if a death is indicated during that year, then Mars coming to the cusp of the eighth would mark the week, probably the day, of the death, while, in that case, the Moon, if it were also in that house, would mark the hour.

Jupiter.—If legacies are promised in the nativity, this is the best position of the great benefic for obtaining them.   Gains

should also come through the partner, of whatever kind. It
tends to produce a more tranquil state of mind, and intuitive
feeling, coming from the higher planes, that everything is
well. If afflicted, there could be losses in connection with
these very things, but it would be more through overconfidence or wastefulness which could be avoided by a little
extra caution at such a time.

Saturn.—In a chart where Saturn is the afflictor there will
certainly be a death of one who is dear to the native, though,
if not afflicted at the time, it will work out in a natural way
and not as a shocking incident. It tends to interest the reasoning individual, and to convince him of the realities of the
planes beyond the material. If afflicted, there could be considerable trouble through the partner and through legacies—
or the affairs of the dead. It is sure to bring one in contact
with death in some definite way.

Uranus.—This brings unsettling conditions into the financial
affairs of the partner and also some unusual experiences from
the astral world. If afflicted—Unexpected and annoying situations may come with regard to money matters. The native
can be put into very difficult situations through the carelessness or erratic action of the partner; through a lawsuit that
may be pending, or some controversy, especially if it has anything to do with a legacy. The unexpected will happen and
certainly not to the benefit of the native.

Neptune.—In the horoscope of a sensitive, psychic person, this
position of Neptune may have an extraordinary effect in the
way of bringing experiences of a very unusual nature. On
the ordinary person it will have but little effect. If afflicted
—It could then be very upsetting, bring confusion and deceit
in regard to the partner's finances, double-crossing or treachery in settling lawsuits or the goods of the dead, and could
prove a sensitive, unhappy time through uncomfortable contact with the astral plane.

THE NINTH HOUSE.

Moon.—This is a good place for the Moon, though, of course,
the transit is of very minor importance. There may be long
flights of thought and imagination.

Mercury.—This stimulates mental energy, though not conducive to concentration, but while Mercury is passing through this house, it is a good time to start new studies, long journeys, and to plan to give, or take, a series of lectures. If afflicted, it will be adverse for the above as the mind will be restless and dissatisfied. Unfavorable, too, for all matters connected with law or lawyers.

Venus.—In a high-class chart it is always good for Venus to be passing through this house. Gives renewed interest in all the arts, fresh ideals and a calmer and more beautiful state of mind. Even in an afflicted chart it will bring very little adversity.

Sun.—The Sun in the ninth makes a good month for all legal procedures, for work with religious bodies, for seeking positions therein and for advancing the position of one working along these lines. Afflicted—Some danger of loss of prestige in connection with such matters.

Mars.—This should stimulate interest in the higher sciences and bring a greater enthusiasm in ideals. If afflicted, it will tend towards arguments, overconfidence and aggressiveness, and a wilder imagination.

Jupiter.—This is good for all matters of philosophy, science or religion. Those who have a well-placed Jupiter should make great strides while Jupiter is transiting through this house, since the mind is clearer and better balanced, the intuition is increased and there are higher aspirations. Both Jupiter and this house have to do with foreign affairs, so that when the aspects are good it makes an excellent time to deal with foreign countries, to take long journeys, and to establish communications. It is also excellent for publications and for handling lawsuits. Afflicted—Care should be taken in all the above matters, for there will be danger of loss, waste or failure due to poor judgment, overenthusiasm or arrogance, particularly applied to litigation.

Saturn.—In a well-aspected chart this brings steadiness of mind and sound philosophic reasoning. Afflicted—Is very adverse for all legal matters, for interviewing lawyers, clergy, professors and partner's brothers and sisters. It tends to bring disputes and coldness and is a very poor time to start any publications, writings or long journeys.

Uranus.—Uranus in this house rarely fails to turn the thoughts to occultism and the higher sciences. It is a splendid place for those who have a nativity that is in sympathy with these things, and everything should be done at such a time as this to cultivate all lines of higher thought, to stimulate the imagination and intuition and to raise the consciousness to a higher level. It is not difficult to do this if one is able to give the right response, for everything is in favor of such advancement and definite progress can be made. Afflicted—An unfavorable time for travel—especially long journeys—for unexpected annoyances and difficulties will present themselves, and there is some danger to health, or life also, if the aspects agree.

Neptune.—A very mystical influence, and one that should be lived up to with the greatest care and earnestness. It can bring inspiration, imagination, vision, clairvoyance and direct contact with the higher planes of consciousness. Afflicted—But if afflicted, it can act as a destructive force, for Neptune in this position may bring great fears, mental unbalance, distorted ideas of the future and a contact with other planes that is very undesirable.

THE TENTH HOUSE.

Moon.—If everything is just right, this will be a good time to make business changes, to travel on business, and to seek honor and preference. It is also good for things that pertain to the mother or to domestic life. Afflicted—Care should be taken in these matters and no changes made.

Mercury.—This is good for all those whose business is along Mercurial lines. It is a good time to buy, sell and deal and to undertake business matters which necessitate signatures, documents and things of similar character. Afflicted—It is adverse for these things and all negotiations should be put off till a later date. Particularly should the native be careful (especially in all matters that have to do with writings or signing papers) if Mercury is retrograding back and forth over the mid-heaven.

Venus.—A very excellent position, especially for those whose ruler it is. Good for entering into lines that pertain to women, to luxuries and adornment, or art. It brings friends in the business world and increased popularity. Afflicted—None of these prophecies will be fulfilled, but not much harm can result.

Sun.—This is also good and, if the Progressed Horoscope agree, it will be a favorable time to seek promotion, to ask for favors from one's employer or from important business men, and it is a good time to start in business for oneself. Afflicted—Care will be needed in all these things, although even in an afflicted nativity this will be the best time for such matters, unless the Sun hits bad aspects at that particular time.

Mars.—For those who respond to the better side of Mars this is a good position, for it gives renewed ambition, enterprise and daring to carry out risky ventures to a successful issue. Afflicted—All kinds of danger can occur from this influence, according to the promise of the nativity. Scandal, ill repute, adverse changes in the business or occupation, and quarrels with business men or employers, as well as rash ventures that will end in a downfall.

Jupiter.—There is no better place in the whole wheel for this great benefic than the mid-heaven. It is not so good for some things as are the other angles, but very favorable for everything in public life. It is an excellent time for marriage, good for the health, and for gaining in honor and reputation. It is still better for all business affairs, for starting new lines, for seeking promotion, for receiving opportunities and for taking advantage of them. Whatever Jupiter brings to the native at this time is more likely to be of permanent benefit than that which comes under any other condition. It brings fame and fortune to those whose nativity permits, and brings credit and the good will of business men. It is favorable for the mother, as well as for domestic and social matters, and increases the popularity. It is under such conditions that we hear of people springing into sudden fame and popularity. Afflicted—It can bring lawsuits, disfavor of the employer, and social disfavor; also may bring loss in business, either through failure, or poor investment, or waste and extravagance, according to the nature of the afflictions.

Saturn.—This position also can bring legal difficulties, but, in a well-aspected chart, they will work out eventually to the benefit of the native, though everything will move very slowly. He will probably attain to some position of trust or responsibility or have some honor conferred upon him or

himself behave with such care and decorum as to receive the
admiration and respect of those with whom he has to deal.
Afflicted—Saturn afflicted in the mid-heaven brings a very
adverse period. Failure, loss, financial and otherwise, trouble
with employers or business associates, misunderstandings,
delays and barriers of all kinds, are some of the things he
will have to contend with. Nothing will go well during
the two years or more that Saturn will take to pass through
this house representing business, profession and honor.

Uranus.—With a strong natal Uranus this position can bring
an increase of power—power of a magnetic character which
is good for those who have close association with other people, especially if it has to do with healing, nursing or teaching. It also stimulates a new interest in occult things, frequently starting a new line of business or profession connected with occultism or with metaphysics. Many astrologers have started out under this aspect. Afflicted—Not at
all good, for it tends to bring about sudden and adverse
changes which alter the whole current of the native's life,
sometimes bringing with it loss of credit and honor and serious financial difficulties.

Neptune.—The effects of Neptune are always more or less
uncertain, but generally they are adverse, because we have
so little power to respond to his high and subtle vibrations
in the right manner. However, in a well-balanced chart with
a strong Mercury, the effect of Neptune passing through the
tenth house should be quite good, and more than likely will
bring some great and totally unexpected benefits, either in
money or some other way according to the natal promises. To
those who have a fortunate nativity it may bring an over-
whelming amount of good fortune, and events of a most mysterious manner will occur and turn to his benefit. Afflicted—
Here we have an opposite condition, for there is danger of all
sorts of reverses, and of everything falling into the most
chaotic condition. There may be insinuations against the
character and reputation coming from sources difficult to
trace; there will be losses through fraud and deception; and
it will not be a good time to take the advice of anyone who
has not been well tested; nor will it be wise to venture into
anything that is not already well established. Vague fears

usually accompany Neptune's afflictions; likewise inertia that comes from a queer mental condition.

Moon.—The position of the Moon here is of little importance, except that it may bring a visit from, or to, a friend. The writer has an astrological friend whom she had not seen for a considerable time and who, one day, phoned to her unexpectedly, asking her to come for a visit. Upon arriving, the friend said: "I am so glad you were able to come, but I was sure you would, because the Moon was transiting the cusp of my eleventh house." Afflicted—Could bring an experience with a fickle friend.

Mercury.—This will bring the more serious type of friends, those who are studious and mental and who will stimulate the native to exercise his own intellectual abilities. Afflicted—It will be well to be careful in dealing with friends, in selling to them, buying from them, or forming any agreements or contracts with them.

Venus.—This, of course, is good and will bring many social activities, pleasant associations, new attachments, love affairs and contact with pretty, artistic and demonstrative people. More particularly will it be women with whom one will be brought into closer association. Afflicted—There will be an excess of emotion and feeling. Not good for making new friends or for social activities.

Sun.—A good place for the Sun, for it helps to bring the native into touch with prominent persons—those who are in a superior position, and those through whom they may receive favors or advancement in position. Afflicted—It will be unfavorable for these things and for the finances of the employer, or for the results of the native's own business.

Mars.—Mars transiting through the eleventh house, which is the house of friends, will bring one in contact with old, or new, friends of the Martial type, and also there will be much activity in regard to one's friends and acquaintances. Afflicted—There will be trouble, quarrels, disputes and enmity.

Jupiter.—This also is good for friendships, especially for establishing good connections with important, influential persons, and those who belong to the clergy, legal profession or foreign service. There are better chances for the realization of one's hopes and wishes than under any other influence. Afflicted—Brings extravagances and profligacy with and through friends, and some waste or heavy expenses through them.

Saturn.—This brings the more serious type of friends—those who are older and have a greater sense of responsibility. They may help the native to look upon life with greater seriousness, and to become more responsible. Afflicted—This will bring difficulties and sorrow through friends, and some ill feeling, coldness or misunderstanding that will take some time to clear up. It could also bring deceit, and the chastening influence of those who might have, or think they have, some authority over the native.

Uranus.—Uranus in the eleventh brings occult friends, an attraction towards some society or brotherhood, a keener interest in philanthropic work and a more unselfish attitude towards humanity. Afflicted—Can bring sudden trouble or estrangements with friends; also trouble with children, more particularly if the native has step-children.

Neptune.—Neptune in this house tends to bring a mysterious element into all one's associations with friends and acquaintances. There will be a greater attraction towards seances, groups of people interested in weird subjects and also towards those who are extremely idealistic and unpractical. Afflicted— There will surely be some deception or treachery among those who are considered friends. There will be double-crossing, intrigue or secrecy and an undercurrent among one's friends that will leave everything vague and unsatisfactory, while considerably later will come the development of all the secrecy and intrigue.

THE TWELFTH HOUSE.

Moon.—Not of great importance unless it is exciting some general directions or important transits, and then more likely to have to do with sickness, food and hygiene than anything else.

Mercury.—Travel to and from sick persons, or those in trouble. Letter writing to the sick, or some communications with hospitals or places of confinement. Afflicted—Treachery through signing papers and agreements. Not a good time to have dealings with people unless everything is clear and aboveboard.

Venus.—This is good and may bring something of a very benefic nature out of a clear sky. Afflicted—Trouble or sorrow through a loved one. The giving up of some thing dearly prized.

Sun.—If the native were properly situated, there could be promotion to the directorship of some institution, a place of honor somewhere, or a contact with important people through whom some unexpected gains could come. Afflicted—An unfavorable time for seeking such things, and not a time to visit hospitals or institutions, or have anything to do with them.

Mars.—Some activities in connection with hospitals or institutions of some kind. Afflicted—False accusations, quarrels, enmity and trouble through secret enemies. Also can bring an operation in a hospital.

Jupiter.—This not infrequently will bring triumph over one's enemies or those who have been, in some way, working indirectly against the native. Afflicted—There will be a bad ending to matters after the native had expected everything to be favorable. The motto "Blessed is he who expecteth nothing, for he shall not be disappointed" is the best for those who have an afflicted Jupiter passing through this house. But when there are no afflictions, really big things may come unsought and unasked, and also unlooked for.

Saturn.—This frequently brings a period of turning back and reviewing life and conditions generally. A checking up, as it were, consideration of making one's will, and putting one's house in order. Everything will take on a more serious aspect and the mind will be more reflective and poised. Afflicted— Sad experiences will come while Saturn is in this house; confinement either through illness, misunderstanding or misbehavior. Sometimes it is solitary confinement, either by being shut off in a lonesome part of the country, or by deceit and treachery, or it may be merely a mental condition which brings loneliness to the soul. To those so inclined there will be melancholia, insomnia, dyspepsia and all sorts of ailments due to nervous depression.

Uranus.—Unexpected things will happen while Uranus is in this house. Good things that are apparently undeserved, queer things, unexpected releases or bonds, and power over one's enemies. Afflicted—This tends to bring disfavor, unexpected calamities, treachery, prosecution, some most unexpected happening that could throw one into prison either through one's own fault, through a misunderstanding, or through the treachery of others, according to the nature of the affliction and the promise of the nativity. Care should be taken in every way to be most circumspect and law-abiding during the years that an afflicted Uranus is passing through this house.

Neptune.—The mysterious, subtle planet, Neptune, passing through this house brings experiences of this nature, and therefore it is most difficult to say just what the reaction will be, but to those who lean towards the spiritual and the occult, great enlightenment and many helpful experiences may occur. Afflicted—The twelfth house is the house of self-undoing— the place where we lay ourselves open to receive the things that are ours from previous incarnations, whether good or ill, and Neptune afflicted in this house will bring many of the ills that are due, which are of that subtle, queer nature that cannot be resisted. It is like the undertow of the ocean—strong, unseen, relentless.

SUMMARY.

It is impossible to tell all the conditions that can come to us through the transits of the planets through the various houses, but, when we understand the nature of the planets and the events that can come through each house, this, together with experience and our intuition, shall reveal to us just what events are likely to come through the various combinations. For instance, the twelfth house rules large animals. So an afflicted malefic passing through the twelfth would bring dangers from that direction. Therefore, if someone were planning to go hunting, it would be logical to warn him of this danger, either advising him not to go or else to use an unusual amount of caution. One man, who has the Sun on the cusp of the twelfth in his nativity in Sagittarius (the sign that rules horses), square to Saturn, was badly trodden upon by a horse at the time that Saturn was transiting through Sagittarius and making adverse aspects, with the Sun coming to the opposition of his own place, and square to the radical Saturn. Others, again, should be warned not to have an operation while there is an afflicted planet in the eighth house, especially if that planet be a malefic, because there would be danger of death under such conditions.

The transits of the planets are exceedingly important, under certain conditions, especially those of the slower-moving planets, but there are times when they will have little or no effect. It is only by very careful study of the Natal Chart, knowing the type of person one is studying, and long years of experience, that one is able to decide how much, or how little, effect the transits are going to have upon the life of a person. The stationary points of the planets, not so much of Mercury and Venus as of the others (unless either planet be their ruler, or stationary at a very sensitive point), are very important and should always be carefully considered. If, for instance, Neptune should stop and change his course, right over a planet, or make a bad aspect to a planet that is afflicted, it will surely bring down upon the native much that was promised in his Natal Chart, and he will pass through some trying experience over which he will have absolutely no control. The only thing to be done in such a case is for him to fortify himself with strength and courage to meet his "fate" and to keep his mind fixed, as far as he is able, on the higher planes. The only way to avoid the difficulties is to endeavor to respond to the vibration of the afflicting planet. For instance, Neptune, being the spiritual planet, thoughts should be directed to the spiritual plane. With Saturn, the planet of reason, we should take time to stop and consider, to be quiet and patient, and *wait*. In this way we are not dodging anything, nor trying to avoid the unpleasant or the difficult, but merely fulfilling our destiny, recognizing our errors and shortcomings, and learning the lessons which life has brought us. It is so simple, if we can but look at it in the right way. There is nothing fantastic about it. It is absolute common sense, and only those who have lived it and proven it know what astrology means to the world. They are the ones who have an understanding of the great *law* that is continually working and who realize that astrology is its practical demonstration.

The majority of us are "of the earth, earthy," and therefore respond more to the Saturnine influence than to any other. While there are many who respond but little to the influences of the two mighty planets Uranus and Neptune, there are none who do not make direct response to the vibrations of Saturn. He is called "The Great Teacher" and his mission is to lay a steadying hand upon us, so that we will take time to stop and consider where we are going, and why. It should be our business, then, to study this planet more than any of the others.

CHAPTER 13.

THE ASPECTS OF THE TRANSITS.

The effects of the progression and transits of the planets through the different signs are similar to the conjunction of the progressed or transiting planet to the ruling planet of the sign it is in. It is hardly necessary to go through all of these, for a thorough knowledge of the basis of astrology should give the student sufficient understanding of this to guide him in the progressed work. It is, of course, impossible to put down on paper all the things that can be known in astrology. Every chart is different; the combination of factors varies in every horoscope so that it is impossible to cover every combination. The best that can be done is to instruct the student in the principles and the methods of reading.

All the transits are more potent when in conjunction with a planet than when they make an aspect, and so, in this section, we will discuss the influences of the transiting planet *over* the other planets, and the student can apply this, modified to some extent, and good or evil, according to the nature of the aspects. For instance, Mars over Mercury will make the mind more acute, sharpen the wits, give quick thoughts and action; perhaps also some journey undertaken on the impulse of the moment, and make a psychological time for the signing of papers or agreements. Unless these planets are afflicting one another at birth, this conjunction will be good, and so also will be the trine and, to a lesser extent, the sextile; but the square or opposition will make it a bad time for signing papers, and the impulses that would come under these vibrations would be unwise to follow. There should be considerable care, at such a time, not to act with any haste, but to wait and consider before doing or saying anything that could have a bearing upon future events.

It should be clearly understood that the transits of, or to, the ruling planet are more potent than any others. They never fail to bring some definite result, either for good or ill, according to the nature of the planet and its aspects and position in the nativity. Unless too heavily afflicted, the tendency

(148)

will always be towards benefits, but it will be in the form that is natural to that planet. For instance, Mars will bring some activity, energy and ambition and the opportunity to act thereon. Saturn will bring a responsibility or mark of esteem; Jupiter and Venus will bring money or the equivalent; the Sun, prestige or honor; Mercury, letters, sales, promises; the Moon, a change or short trip; Uranus, a surprise or sudden event; and Neptune, some inspiration or psychic experience. This is in reference to the ruler of the rising sign.

The transits of any of the planets over their own places tend to awaken all that is promised by the planets through their aspects, signs and positions. This marks a very important period if the planet is strong at birth, and such transits should be noted with care, especially if the planet should be stationary on that point. Venus passing over her own place in the tenth should bring benefits along the lines of the native's business or profession, and greater activity among women than men. Mars in the tenth would bring general activities in business and, if afflicted, would bring trouble with employer, and an impulsive change. And so on, with each house and planet.

Each planet stands for, or represents, a certain part of man's character, and the strength and importance of any planet gives the key to the dominant characteristic of the individual; while the reverse is also true, that the confinement or weakness of a planet will indicate the weak or morbid spot in the native's character. Mars represents force and action, and his contact with the other planets brings an issue of some kind, because in his action he naturally "collides" with some other force. If the planet is Mercury, the issue lies in argument, quarrel, dispute or, if well aspected, in teaching someone else. If it is with Venus, there is issue of feelings. Love at first sight comes from the aspect of these two, so that immediately there is an issue to face. With Saturn, it is an issue with an older person; with Uranus, a clash of will; and so on.

Venus is centripetal in her action and draws everything to herself. She tries to soften and harmonize everything so as to avoid an issue and thus gets her name for love and harmony. Every time Mercury touches another planet she stimulates the mental faculties, induces thought and brings adaptability. Jupiter represents expansion, and this gives the appearance of nobility and generosity in the native; while Saturn acts in exactly the opposite way and teaches economy, conservation, chastity and concentration. Uranus is the out-law; he will obey no law, not even those of his own making. He considers rules were made to break and is a law unto himself, acting just as his erratic feelings will suggest. Will power directed against him has little or no effect. And Neptune is just the opposite, allowing every condition, environment and all people to impress him and affect his action.

Another thing to be remembered with regard to the transits is, that while we have given the effects of the quicker-moving planets over the slower, it is the slow-moving planets that have the greatest influence. For instance, the Sun over Saturn shows trouble with employer, or in business and finance. It also shows poor health, but this will last but a day, perhaps, while the transit of Saturn over the Sun will continue anywhere from a week to a month or two, so that the student must always make allowances for the time that is taken to transit, or aspect, another planet.

Mars is the planet of force, heat and energy, so it should always be remembered that when he contacts another planet he imbues it with a certain amount of his own qualities, since he is so very positive. When Mars is afflicted in a nativity, his transit over, square, or opposition, to a planet will be malefic, and care should be taken against impulsive actions and hasty speech. But in those charts where Mars is weak, the transits over a planet will be good, for they will tend to stir up action and force in a character that is rather lacking in those necessary qualities. Let us suppose that a Natal Chart contains Mars in Aries, conjoined with the Moon. We will know that that person is very impulsive, easily stirred to anger, and of quick, imprudent speech, so that every transit of either of these two planets to that place will awaken such tendencies, and he will be continually saying and doing the rash or wrong thing in the wrong place. But should Mars be weakly placed in Libra and making no important aspects of any kind, then his transits will be of use in rousing the person who has not naturally sufficient fight, energy or enterprise; and even the square and opposition will have a some-what good effect.

MARS.

Mars over Venus.—This usually brings a new attraction or friendship with one of the opposite sex and greater activity in all social affairs; also a vacation or some form of active pleasure. Afflicted—It brings extravagance, loss through women, or quarrels with them, and some expressions of vanity.

Mars over Mercury tends towards a decided increase in mental energy. The mind will work quicker, matters that have been awaiting signatures will come to a head, and there may be a journey, or some renewed activities in regard to correspondence or papers. Mars over Mercury makes for an over-active brain, some danger of nervous exhaustion, sharp speech and anger, unless very well aspected, when it will be good for making new plans, for work that requires a keen and critical mind, and for actions daring in their nature. Afflicted—It will act in much the same way, but with unfavorable results. One should be much more careful in signing papers or documents, and should not allow the mind to work too fast, because, to those so inclined, it could cause too much excitement and nervousness. It will be unfavorable for buying or selling. There is also danger of quarrels, criticisms and sarcasm.

Mars over the Sun will bring activities in business, dealings with men of importance and influence, and possibly opportunities for advancement, or a new position. Afflicted—Not good for the health, because there will be too much activity, too much blood and heat, and the main thing is to be calm and do something of a quiet, serious nature. An overheated brain and body brings danger of quarrels, rashness, sickness and regrettable actions.

Mars over the Moon frequently brings some quick change, a journey, or business activity. Afflicted—Is not good for such things and brings danger of disputes in regard to them, especially in matters that have to do with females.

Mars over Jupiter.—This should bring activity in business, some success in financial matters, and even in social affairs. The vibrations are often an incentive to buying machinery, automobiles and such things and also bring ninth house affairs into play. Afflicted—Causes heavy expenditures, some extravagance, waste, loss, disputes over finances, and legal difficulties.

Mars over Saturn is not good at all, or very rarely. Sometimes it will prove beneficial to those who are naturally too quick and impulsive, because the rashness of Mars is modified by the steadiness of Saturn, but it is more inclined to act like fire and water and cause a blowup. Resentment comes into play, smoldering anger directed towards elderly people or superiors, and often there is trouble with an employer or the father. It also brings danger of accidents.

Mars over Uranus.—This also tends towards accidents, as in fact do all the afflictions of Mars, and the conjunction of these two planets is always considered an affliction. It is explosive in its nature, and causes accidents such as gunshots, explosions by gunpowder, blowing fuses, and other electrical accidents. It brings nervous affections, quick anger, quarrels, rash actions, and things done on the spur of the moment that can cause regret immediately afterwards. In a very high-class chart it may stimulate the intuition and the mental faculties and give more will power and magnetic force. Afflicted—The same conditions will prevail, but they will be much worse— that is, they will cause a person to commit one of the terrible things that are so often recorded in the newspapers—murders, assaults, etc; and if either planet be in the twelfth house, it will eventually land them in confinement.

Mars over Neptune tends to increased interest in all Neptunian things; it gives inspiration in music, art or drama, and stimulates any activities that have to do with liquids, oils, tobacco, and narcotics and stimulants of various kinds. Afflicted—It is adverse for all these things and, like the aspects to Uranus, is of a more or less violent nature, causing accidents, harm to the native through other persons, assaults, treachery and so forth.

VENUS.

Venus over Mercury brings a very pleasant vibration, stimulating friendships and bringing pleasures, music, fun and short trips. It is a good time for correspondence, especially in regard to such things, and for dealing with agents, buying, selling and trading. Afflicted—The affliction can never be very bad, unless these planets afflict one another at birth; and then it is bad for all the above or for the things signified by the position of the two planets in the Natal Chart.

Venus over the Sun.—Is exceedingly good. It is fast moving and therefore soon over, but unless there are heavy afflictions, it never fails to bring something definite and good. It may be just a gift of flowers, or candy, or an invitation of an attractive nature—more to do with social life than domestic; or else, if it is a person in business, it will be a day when some good fortune will come. There may be more customers in the store, money may come in more freely, and all things work out smoothly and pleasantly. Afflicted—Is more likely to be negative, instead of some active good, as in the case of benefic vibrations, but in a very heavily afflicted chart it will bring disappointment, expenses and trouble through women, or through one's affections.

Venus over the Moon is also good, but not quite so powerful, and has more to do with domestic life and contacts with women than with those things which belong to out-door life or business. It is good for finances, but on the whole, is more likely to bring pleasures, visitors and gifts into the home than to work out in other ways. Afflicted—May bring some little unpleasantness into the home, or some additional expense. Cannot do much harm.

Venus over Jupiter brings the two benefics together, and is, naturally, very good. But there is danger of its being *too* good and causing excess or overindulgence or extravagance. Apart from that, it is entirely beneficial, and usually works more through the finances than in any other way. This is one of the few cases where the trine and sextile will act more definitely and wholly for good than the conjunction in the transits. Afflicted—Can do very little harm, but will sometimes bring a financial loss, or lessen expected profits; is not so good for social affairs and friendships.

Venus over Saturn helps to establish more permanent affections. Will bring love or friendship from some older person, and is good for dealings with men in responsible positions. A good deal depends, of course, as with all the other planets, on the house and sign in which the transit takes place. It can also be beneficial in business and financial affairs. Afflicted—There will be disappointments, sorrow, coldness or misunderstandings with a friend, and it is quite unfavorable for any love affairs, or matters in which the affections are involved.

Venus over Uranus also has to do with the affections, bringing some surprise, new love affair or very unusual friendship. The kind of thing that happens under this configuration is such as a last-minute decision to go down a certain street and meeting some person whom one may afterwards marry, or become very closely associated with in some other capacity. It is good also for business or profession. Afflicted—The same kind of events may occur, but they end unsatisfactorily, and ties or friendships that are already established will be broken.

Venus over Neptune also has to do with friendships and love affairs. But they will be more on the order of platonic friendships, or something quite out of the usual. The transit will also bring some very pleasant trip, picnic, or social event. Afflicted—Brings about much the same conditions, but in an unsatisfactory way, attended by scandal, loss or disappointment.

MERCURY.

Mercury over the Sun is good for business transactions, employment, starting on journeys, or new plans, and is also good for all kinds of literary work and teaching. Afflicted—Makes it unfavorable for these things, for buying or selling, or transacting any kind of business.

Mercury over the Moon tends to bring about a short journey, or some kind of a change in the home, and is good for all matters of writing, correspondence and lectures. Afflicted—Will make it unfavorable for changes, journeys or writings.

Mercury over Jupiter is very good, especially for all legal matters, for those things which require careful judgment and clear thought and for all who are engaged in literary work. It helps also in social life, and in bringing success or recognition. The mind should be clearer and more peaceful, and at the same time more buoyant. Afflicted—Is bad for litigation and indicates a time when all matters requiring careful consideration and keen judgment should be postponed. Not good for dealings with relatives by marriage.

Mercury over Saturn.—This causes mental depression, despondency, fretting, and anxiety—even though the planets be well aspected. It can work out for good because it brings the desire to stop and think and to go over things carefully —to take stock, as it were, which helps to steady the mind and give greater concentration. It gives a steadier flow of speech and may even give eloquence to those with a natural ability for speaking and lecturing. Afflicted—This gives real despondency and depression that is hard to overcome. Also bad for signing papers, for correspondence and for trading. There will be delays or anxiety over mail, and it is a very poor time for starting any journey or new undertaking.

Mercury over Uranus.—Quickens the mentality; gives originality and greater intuition. A good time for starting studies along occult or metaphysical lines and for doing work that requires constructive ingenuity. Afflicted—Brings mental trouble, adversities in the things mentioned above, and estrangements with friends, brothers and sisters.

Mercury over Neptune.—This also increases the intuition and is very good for those who write or do any creative work, since it gives inspiration and visions. Afflicted—Gives distorted views, premonitions and vague fears. There will be queer notions and ideas that cannot be relied upon, and to those who are naturally nervous and sensitive it will bring a strain and may cause a complete breakdown, if other vibrations agree.

SUN.

Sun over the Moon.—Is good if neither are afflicted in the nativity. It will bring an unimportant change of some kind. A good time to start new undertakings and to make new friends. Afflicted—It is bad for the health of a woman and is quite unfavorable for all domestic affairs.

Sun over Jupiter.—Especially good, and should bring promotion, a good offer, or some opportunity. It is good for business, dealing with superiors and employers, and for asking favors and seeking rewards. Afflicted—Indicates loss or disfavor along the lines of the business or profession. It is adverse for dealings with superiors or employers, and is no time for investing or for financing.

Sun over Saturn.—Steadies and slows up all proceedings. If very well aspected it may bring some honor or responsibility; otherwise it tends to depression, delay and responsibilities. Usually the native has a keener sense of duty, orderliness and precision. Afflicted—This is very hard on the native, for it tends towards ill health, trouble with superiors, loss of position, reputation, or money, and a great many obstacles and hindrances.

Sun over Uranus.—Causes the unexpected to happen. Sudden changes in business, sudden developments with those in authority, an unexpected rise in status, and greater power and magnetism. Afflicted—It can bring disgrace, trouble with superiors, loss of reputation, and a change in occupation, and ill health.

Sun over Neptune.—Causes a state of restlessness and uncertainty. When very well aspected, there can be benefits through dealings in oils, oil wells, or leases, with liquids of any kind, and gains through "hunches." Afflicted—It is quite evil, bringing adverse changes of a kind indicated by the position and aspects of these two in the nativity. It tends towards confusion, delusion, intrigue and chaos, mentally, emotionally and in mundane affairs.

It is not necessary to give the effects of the transiting Moon over the planets, because it moves so fast that there is no certainty that it will strike a planet at the time when its actions may be felt. For instance, the Moon might pass over Mercury at four o'clock in the morning. The aspect induces study, reading, interviews or a walk. But at that time in the morning most people would be oblivious to the vibrations and make no response. There are times when the Moon aspecting a sensitive planet like Neptune can cause an unusually vivid dream or a psychic experience, but the transiting Moon's aspects are so dependent upon the others prevailing that they cannot be relied upon to have the natural effects. We have, however, known of specially remunerative business being consummated when the Moon passed over Venus or Jupiter in the mid-heaven, and have noted similar results from other houses, but these cannot be depended upon to bring the expected action every time.

JUPITER.

Jupiter over the Moon.—Good for all things that have to do with the home and domestic life, for the mother and for social life. It will often bring about a friendship with a woman that will be very beneficial in afterlife, and brings expansion in many ways in the private life of the individual. Afflicted— Tends towards some loss or trouble in the home, but it is not a very serious matter at any time, unless the horoscope is an unusually afflicted one from other directions as well.

Jupiter over Saturn will frequently bring promotion or gain through older people, superiors or employers. There may be gain also through property, and it is a good time to make permanent those particular things that are at the time the most desirable. Afflicted—Can bring considerable loss to the native; loss through discredit, of favor, of position, or through investments and inability to handle the conditions in which the native may find himself.

Jupiter over Uranus.—Brings unexpected good luck, a regular windfall, and is especially fortunate for those who are working in science, philosophy or law. Good for lawsuits or litigation of any kind. Afflicted—There is danger of loss—sudden and unexpected—perhaps loss of position or authority, and is very unfavorable for investments or speculation.

Jupiter over Neptune.—Tends to bring an expansion of consciousness. It is good for business and worldly things, but more so for those which have to do with art and music; often brings popularity, pleasures and friendships with those interested in occultism and the higher lines of thought. Afflicted— Brings intrigue in matters connected with law or lawsuits, double-crossing, unpopularity, and loss from the directions through which the aspects come.

SATURN.

Saturn over the Moon.—Even in a favorable chart this configuration inclines to trouble in domestic affairs. In a woman's chart it will bring ill health and lowered vitality and it is rarely that it does not bring disappointment in family matters and losses in business. Afflicted—It will bring a death or much sickness, also delays and opposition in the affairs indicated by the houses which are involved.

Saturn over Uranus.—Often brings the native to the notice of the public, which will look upon him with greater favor or give him some position of authority or responsibility. He will have more power and strength within himself and should be able to command others. Afflicted—It will work in almost exactly the opposite manner. There will be loss of reputation, loss of public favor, separations or humiliations and trouble with, or through, superiors or in some other way indicated by the position of these planets in the Radical Chart.

URANUS.

Uranus over the Moon.—Trouble with mother, wife or some other female. Disturbances or upheavals in family matters and very unsettled conditions in the home. A change of some kind is inevitable and, excepting in a very favorable chart, it will prove an unsatisfactory one. If the horoscope is a very afflicted one, there will be separations, estrangements, divorce or something of that nature which will make a radical change in the life of the native.

Uranus over Neptune.—Is a peculiar and unusual configuration. It is a very powerful vibration; too strong for some people to stand up under, and thus creates confusion and chaos in their minds and lives. It is good for those who pursue uncommon lines of work, who work along occult or psychic lines, and much knowledge and insight may be obtained while these two are together. It may be a very strenuous time, but well worth while going through for those who want to become acquainted with life and progress to the higher planes. Afflicted—It will bring strange and trying experiences, many of them belonging to the occult or psychic planes. There may be loss through lack of understanding, or confusion of mind, and everything will seem to be unsettled, unsatisfactory, changeable, in a turmoil and generally most trying. It is impossible to say just what could happen, but all sorts of disagreeable situations could arise to make things difficult and unpleasant for the native, and the only thing to do is to keep as quiet as possible, to avoid trying to do anything with or through the public, and to keep from dabbling in psychism.

NEPTUNE.

Neptune over the Moon.—This will bring confusion, intrigue and anxiety into the home affairs and with all domestic relations. At this time care should be taken in all dealings with others, but particularly in the home circle and no changes made unless everything works out in a natural and open manner. Much afflicted it will bring treachery, unsatisfactory business dealings and trouble with property.

All adverse aspects to the Moon, from any of the planets, and in any part of the horoscope, will incline to ill health in a female chart or to upset the domestic life in some manner.

CHAPTER 14.

EXAMPLE.

Female born October 31, 1892, at 10:44 a. m.; latitude 39.40 N., longitude 105 W.

As indicated in the preceding chapters, before the effect of progressions can be determined, the character, general tendencies, etc., must be sought in the Radical Chart.

In this example the Radical Chart shows a person who has a strong character, is selfish and temperamental. One who is insistent, persistent and self-willed. Clever, versatile, high-strung and perceptive. (Sun in Scorpio conjunct Uranus, with the ruler of Scorpio—Mars, square to Mercury.) Her imagination is fertile and very active and she has written charming little poems and lyrics. (Mercury in Scorpio sextile Venus in Virgo.) Mercury in Scorpio gives her perception, makes her keenly critical, while Mercury square to Mars makes her a fault-finder. Selfish and lazy—Sagittarius rising and the Moon in Pisces—she wants something for nothing all the time. The best only is good enough for her. She desires ease and luxuries and is indifferent as to the means used to obtain them.

Self-deception plays an important part in her life—Moon square Neptune—so no matter how wrong she might be, or how desirous of something to which she is not entitled, she can always make it appear as though her desires are legitimate, and prove—at any rate to herself—that the other fellow is not doing his part and she is being done out of that which is rightfully hers. It is extraordinary to what lengths she will go in this regard. The strength and determination of the Sun conjoined with Uranus in Scorpio, the square of Mercury in Scorpio to Mars, and the square of the Moon in Pisces to Neptune gives the keynote to the character and every action and reaction hinges upon these three centers of force. This throws light on the succeeding events in her life. Had she been of a different character; had her natural reactions been different, her life would be altogether different and very much happier; that is, as far as we can see. Only some of the events of her

(160)

EXAMPLE 161

life are known to me, though I am now going to read the horoscope roughly right through life in order to illustrate the methods of progression according to the natural tendencies of the nativity.

She has a lovely side to her. She is, to begin with, very handsome; Sagittarius rising and Venus in Virgo sextile Mercury, and she keeps herself beautifully groomed. In fact, money is often spent on her personal appearance when it is due elsewhere. It never occurs to her that her personal needs should not come first of all, not even if it means the sacrifice of her child. She has personal charm and people are quickly attracted to her; the Moon in Pisces trine the Sun and Uranus in Scorpio. She has never been able to hold any friends because of her selfishness, her deceitfulness and her fault-finding, but she has made many friends and has had popularity and admiration many times.

Men are attracted to her and when she cares to exert her charms she can be very fascinating, but because of her constant demands she cannot maintain, for any long time, fascination over those whom she desires to charm. She is a great lover of nature; Sagittarius rising and the Moon in Pisces. She enjoys a home and keeps it up beautifully; so many planets in watery signs gives her the love of home and Venus in Virgo gives the desire for keeping it in perfect order and her love for simple country life and communion with nature.

Being a woman of strong character and much power (Sun, Uranus and Mercury all in Scorpio), when once she realizes what she is doing she will be able to change her character and start to develop that side of it that tends towards nobility, graciousness and kindliness.

At the age of 12 and 13 years Venus progressed to a trine of Neptune, Mercury to an opposition of Neptune and the transiting Uranus crossed the ascendant, so that if the girl had been a little older it would have been natural to suppose that her life was exceedingly eventful, bringing love affairs, intrigue, peculiar conditions, unusual happenings and maybe a sudden marriage. Since she was too young for such things, corresponding events would occur more likely to affect the parents or bring conditions in her environment which, while having some effect upon her, would not necessarily work out in any personal way involving strain or change upon her personally. Therefore, the first period of importance would be at the age of 14 years, when the Sun came to a conjunction with Mercury, the progressed Mercury to a sextile with the progressed Venus and the Moon progressed over Saturn.

The transits at that time were Neptune and Uranus opposing one another, the former trine the Sun and Uranus and the latter sextile to the same two planets. These progressions and transits indicate that she had an opportunity to make her way in the world. Her mind would be more active than it had ever been and she would plan to do things for herself for her own personal benefit in the way in which she has continued to do ever since. The Sun conjunct Mercury would produce an active mental state, and though she has had no chance to have more than an ordinary education, she would be able to use what she had to secure a place in the business world if she so desired. She no doubt did this, for I know she had to work at an early age and was very mature for her years, appearing already grown up when just entering the adolescent period.

That she would be popular and a success is seen by the sextile of Mercury and Venus, Venus being elevated above all the other planets in the horoscope by this time. She would have greater facilities for expression and be able to use her beauty and her charms to the best advantage. Domestic troubles would beset her at this time and would be one of the reasons for it being necessary for her to find employment. Domestic troubles, so long as they did not affect her personally, would not have great weight with her, and since the Venus aspects were good, she would receive admiration and attention, so that the necessity of getting out would not be a trial to her.

The cause of the domestic troubles is seen by progressed Mercury square Moon, the transiting planets, Neptune and Uranus, in opposition to one another, both making squares to her Saturn, while Saturn and Jupiter both afflict the natal Moon and Neptune. Thus we would judge that the

EXAMPLE   163

father, represented by Saturn, was undergoing a very difficult time, as was also her mother, who is represented by the Moon.

The native's mother would have a much sadder and more harassed life than the father because the Moon has the heavy affliction to Neptune, but as this luminary had just passed the trine to Uranus and the Sun, the native would have a stronger tie and sympathy with the mother, though the father would maintain a more prominent place in her life, probably demanding more of her and outliving the mother by a wide margin.

From this time the following two or three years would be a period involving much deception, a great deal of jealousy and some very trying situations. The reason for this is because the Sun proceeds immediately to a square with Mars, awakening to the fullest extent the square of Mercury and Mars at the time of birth. As this involves something inherent in the native's character, it would bring to the surface some of her worst qualities and so give her a chance to overcome them and get them out of her system. In the light of future events she apparently did not accomplish this, so it may be presumed that these influences worked out in many little deceits, concealments, untruths, etc., as to the source of her income, or in some other direction, according to lines along which her life was laid, her immediate needs and her immediate temptations.

Financial difficulties, of course, would present themselves, due to the fact that Mars is on the cusp of the second house, the house of money, especially during the latter part of 1907 and throughout 1908, because of the afflictions of Jupiter to the natal Sun and Uranus, Mercury and Mars.

At 17 she married under the directions Sun square Mars, sextile Venus with Venus opposition Jupiter and the transiting Uranus and Neptune square Venus and Jupiter from the progressed first and progressed seventh houses respectively, while the transiting Saturn in Aries was conjunct Jupiter. Great knowledge of astrology is not necessary to predict that marriage under such conditions could not last. It will be noted at a glance that the nativity of this woman does not promise a happy marriage. First, the Sun is in close conjunction with Uranus, always a sure sign, in a woman's chart, of separations and estrangements; then the Moon, ruling domestic affairs, is square to Neptune, bringing chaotic conditions into the home, while the ruler of the seventh, Mercury, is in close square to Mars, which tends to quarrels, unguarded speech and friction.

The chart also indicates a person of extreme selfishness—one with no thought beyond herself—self comes first, last and at all times. Because of this she is not able to overcome the adverse influences concerning marriage. Had she more self-control, did she not demand so much from others and so little of herself, she could have had a different life. As it is, she reacts to every passing vibration; in other words, allows the influences from the planets to dominate her life with apparently no effort to prevent them.

It was the opposition, in 1909, of the progressed Venus to Jupiter, Venus ruling the fifth house, the house of love affairs, which brought the love affair which culminated in marriage. The progressed aspects of the Sun indicate the marriage, while the transit of Uranus over the progressed Ascendant precipitated the event just when she was 17. Uranus with the Sun in the nativity has a powerful influence in marriage, but even without this relation to the Sun he may be a factor, especially when crossing the Ascendant, in which case marriage is usually precipitous, made under some unusual conditions, and sometimes because of some irregularities. The aspects of the transiting planets and of the progressed Venus and natal Jupiter directed to the first and seventh angles was another indication that marriage was imminent, and, both because of the promise of the nativity and the transits and progressions, it was what one might term an inevitable experience.

At the time of the marriage the progressed Moon had just passed from a conjunction of Uranus and the Sun, and had almost come to the trine of the natal Moon. Thus: the progression of the Sun indicated the year of the marriage, the progressed Moon the part of that year, while the New Moon in November, together with the transits, set that month as the momentous time. This marriage ended in disaster within

EXAMPLE   165

eighteen months, when Saturn and Jupiter transited in opposition to one another, hitting the natal Sun and Uranus. Mars
progressed to a trine with the natal Uranus and Sun, from
the house of money, gave her the chance to earn her own
living after the divorce, which she did on both the legitimate
stage and in the movies. Both a public life and an artistic
one is seen by Venus ruling the mid-heaven and at that time
progressing to a semi-sextile with Mercury and then to a
trine with Mars, while Mercury was all that time sextile
progressed Venus and going to a sextile with Mars. There
is indication of many ups and downs during those few years
following the divorce, for the transits of Uranus and Saturn
would bring many unpleasantnesses and make her glad to
abandon a public career for that of an easy married life, free
from the anxieties entailed in earning her own living.

During 1910 she no doubt experienced a great deal of pleasure and happiness, because the progressed Sun was sextile to
Venus, while the transiting Uranus was close to a trine to
Venus and sextile the progressed Sun, but the fact that
Uranus was involved in the vibrations at the time would tend
to stir up the inharmonies indicated in the Natal Chart.* Indications of matrimonial trouble can be seen in the aspects of
Neptune square progressed Venus, and Jupiter transiting
over Saturn, for she is the type that would resent authority,
refusing to recognize anyone as superior to herself.

There would be popularity and much promise through her
improved social position, due to the trine of Jupiter to Neptune. Jupiter working his way gradually toward the mid-
heaven over the progressed Venus and to the sextile of the
progressed Mercury and trine Mars would greatly please her
vanity, bringing to her during the late fall many little
triumphs and gratifications. The effect of this would be to
make her more selfish and indifferent to the duties of her
household, and so, during the winter months, the adverse
influences generated when the progressed Moon came to a
conjunction of Mercury and a square with the natal Mars
would affect adversely her domestic and marital relationships.
Then Jupiter transiting over the Sun and Uranus, while an

---

*See last two paragraphs of Chapter 3.

excellent configuration at certain times and under certain conditions, would in this case increase the egoism and self-assertiveness, while Saturn in opposition to all these would add fuel to the fire.

Much unhappiness would come throughout the winter of 1911-12, for at that time the progressed Moon was in opposition to Neptune and square to her own natal place, while the transiting Mars was stationary in exact conjunction with Neptune and opposition the progressed Moon, and then retrograded to a position almost exactly opposite the natal Mercury and square to his own natal place. This would all be so disturbing, especially since Jupiter was involved in the same squares and oppositions throughout the winter. Her health would be attacked and she would face heavy expenditures and many vexing problems. Ill health through the Lunar and Mars aspects; expenses through Jupiter, and both of these tending to upset the regular routine and harmony of life.

Of course there were many compensating influences and she would be able to get through with the help of friends, by her own determination and through good luck, which would come through many good aspects to Venus and Mercury.

In August, 1911, a daughter was born. The progressed Sun had just passed the sextile to Venus while Uranus was in exact trine to Venus and therefore close to the sextile of the progressed Sun and on the day of the birth, the 20th, the transiting Venus was over Venus trine Uranus, sextile the progressed Sun. The Moon was trine to the Sun and Uranus, Neptune was sextile to Mercury, but Mars and Saturn were conjoined close to the opposition to Mercury and square Mars from the fifth house. Because of the aspects of Mars and Saturn, had her condition in life been less favorable, she might have lost the child and in any case, later in life, there would undoubtedly be much trouble for the child, and in connection with her. This, in fact, proved to be the case. The child was neglected and suffered through loneliness and a lack of right training and opportunity.

In 1912, after the divorce, she would be on her feet again with the advantages brought to her by the sextile of Jupiter

Example   167

to Saturn, but there would be some deprivations and a good deal of mental depression and resentment due to the transit of Saturn opposition Mercury and square to Mars.

The year 1913 would be hard in many ways, because, lacking help from the progressed Sun, the transiting Uranus square to his own place and close to the square of the Sun, and Saturn transiting over Neptune, square the natal Moon, are both rather disrupting influences and would naturally stimulate a desire for a change of conditions. Her desire would be toward marriage, undoubtedly, both because this would be her natural reaction and also because the Sun, the marriage pointer in a woman's horoscope, had just progressed into a new sign, signifying changes of considerable import to the individual. There would appear to be opportunities for marriage, Jupiter sextile the Sun and Uranus, and sextile Moon during a large part of the year, but they would come to naught while Saturn was square to the Moon.

In regard to love affairs and marriage, 1914 would present much the same conditions and problems, with Uranus then transiting a square of the Sun, but opportunities would prove elusive. No sooner started than ended in some extraordinary manner. Nothing cohesive or settled. She could carry out no plans during those months, for it would be next to impossible for matters to turn out the way planned. Disappointments, delays and deprivations of one kind and another, much due to ill-health or depression of mind and body, for Saturn still transiting square to the Moon would cause everything to lag and be at a standstill.

In 1915 there would be better conditions in every way. Saturn trine the natal Sun and Moon, Neptune trine the progressed Sun, and Jupiter transiting over the Moon, trine Mercury and sextile the Ascendant, would bring a love affair with a promise of a better ending than the others, so that, finally, in 1916, after she had passed her twenty-third birthday, marriage would take place under better conditions by far than the first venture. This time the love planet Venus was the dominating influence, bringing both the love affair and the marriage. She had progressed to a conjunction of the mid-heaven, trine Mars, but square to the progressed Ascendant. Progressed Mars was trine the natal Sun. These aspects are infinitely better than those which brought the first marriage, and therefore the good influences were sufficient for her to have made a success of this venture had she been of an unselfish character and more interested in keeping harmony than in the gratification of her own desires.

The man she married at this time was a very fine type, handsome, kindly and generous. He legally adopted the little girl, the product of the first marriage, and did his best for her. He was a money-maker and had a more than adequate income, with prospects of considerably more when his father died. All this was very nice as far as it went, but it was not sufficient for this lady. She wanted more and more, demanded more of her husband than he had strength or time for, during the evenings after a hard business day, and gradually she became fault-finding and dissatisfied. All went well for some time, for she had everything she would wish, nothing to do that she did not wish to do, a good home provided for her little girl, and money on which to dress as well as one would wish, in reason. Satisfaction, however, soon gave place to discontent, since Uranus, during the first part of 1917, was stationary square to Mercury, remaining close there all the year and towards the winter Neptune became stationary square to Uranus, and Saturn transiting in conjunction with Neptune was square to both Uranus and the Sun. The benefits were too many to cause her to wish a change at this time, but the feeling of dissatisfaction would be there just the same, and throughout 1918 would be even more pronounced, since Uranus would be over Mars, square Mercury; Neptune square to the Sun as well as to Uranus, and Saturn arriving before the end of the year at a square with Mercury, and opposition of Mars and opposition the transiting Uranus. At this time she received a slight accident to her spine, which has caused her trouble at times ever since. The favorable influences of Jupiter trine the Sun and Uranus kept things going along pretty well on the surface.

The year 1922 brought strenuous vibrations: Progressed Mercury square Venus, and Mars square Neptune, Uranus transiting over the Moon, square Neptune. Having nothing better to occupy her mind, she fancied herself in love with another man, and with still greater flight of fancy thought he

EXAMPLE   169

was willing to divorce his wife to marry her, though of this he had no intention. In spite of all advice and much distress on the part of her husband she insisted upon a divorce and, finally, in 1923, had her way (progressed Sun opposition Neptune, progressed Uranus conjunct Sun, progressed Mars conjunct Moon and progressed Venus conjunct Uranus). It was impossible to make her see that she was not an abused person. She lacked judgment (Sun opposition Neptune) and so she ruined at least three lives, at any rate for the time being.

Her ex-husband later married again and this time to a woman who made a real home for him and gave him much-desired children, so that for him, in the end, it was a distinct benefit. The woman, as may be expected, was not long in realizing what she had done, and bitterly regretted her impulse. She did her best to get the divorced husband to remarry her, and for a time he appeared to be considering this. It seemed afterwards, however, that he was merely endeavoring to stall court action for what she thought adequate alimony. Then, suddenly, without giving her any intimation of a change of mind, he announced his marriage to the other woman. In the native's Progressed Chart the Sun was opposition Neptune, which indicated this duplicity.

All this time and for several years afterwards, progressed Venus was over Uranus and the Sun, and thus began a series of love affairs, in the attempt to secure another husband. All of these attempts ended in some peculiar and unexpected manner, much to her chagrin. For a time life was nothing but confusion, disappointment and loss and has continued more or less so up to the present time. Presently, however, there should be a distinct change, for the progressed Sun is nearing a trine of the natal Jupiter, Mercury sextile Mars and Venus trine the Moon. This should bring an opportunity to marry to advantage, possibly a real love match, at any rate for the time being, and should also bring mental expansion and a better and more healthy outlook on life.

Prosperity will come through the Sun trine Jupiter, the love match through Venus trine the Moon and the changed mental attitude through Mercury sextile Mars. During much of 1931 Uranus will be in transit over Jupiter, trine progressed Sun, and Neptune sextile Sun and Uranus, which might easily precipitate a third marriage. During 1932, however, with Uranus stationary in exact conjunction with the fourth cusp and Neptune square his own place and later going to the opposition of the natal Moon, she is likely to get into an unreasonable state of mind similar to that which possessed her when the Sun opposed Neptune, and this would again break up all chances for continued happiness. If the nativity were not one of fault-finding and continual demands (Mercury in Scorpio square Mars), it is possible that this woman could adjust herself to the needs and rights of others and thus be happy in marriage. As it is, assuredly she is making evident the truism, "Character is Destiny."